J. WESTON
WALCH
PUBLISHER
Portland, Maine

Content-Area Research Strategies

Language Arts

Mathematics

Social Studies

Science

Kate O'Halloran

User's Guide
to
Walch Reproducible Books

Purchasers of this book are granted the right to reproduce all pages.

This permission is limited to a single teacher, for classroom use only.

Any questions regarding this policy or requests to purchase further reproduction rights should be addressed to

Permissions Editor
J. Weston Walch, Publisher
321 Valley Street • P.O. Box 658
Portland, Maine 04104-0658

1   2   3   4   5   6   7   8   9   10

ISBN 0-8251-4488-4

Printed in the United States of America

Contents

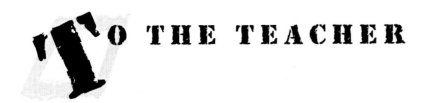

TO THE TEACHER

For many students, research projects are a leap in the dark. They know they must produce a paper, but they're not really sure how to go about it. Most teenagers have little knowledge of the information-seeking process. And while a written paper is the finished product, writing is only half the battle. Before students can start to write, they must first plan, research, and organize their material. These activities call for skills that many students have not learned.

The lessons in *Content-Area Research Strategies* will help fill in the blanks. This book breaks the entire research process down into its composite steps, from choosing a research topic through taking notes and preparing a bibliography, to revising the finished research paper.

The skills students learn in the course of these lessons will also benefit them in other ways. Studies suggest that teaching students such skills as writing summary paragraphs, organizing and categorizing materials, and outlining information leads to improved academic performance, better retention of information, and increased reading comprehension.

The research process is presented in this book in a step-by-step manner: choosing a topic, narrowing the topic, identifying the main topics for research, finding and evaluating resources, reading for research, taking notes, recording bibliographic information, organizing notes, preparing an outline, writing and revising the paper, and preparing the bibliography. These steps will provide students with a structure they can use for researching and organizing information in any context.

Classroom Management   *Content-Area Research Strategies* is easy to use. Simply photocopy each lesson and distribute it. Each lesson focuses on one step in the process and includes models showing the step in context. Some lessons include graphic organizers to show students ways to approach the material. Blank copies of these graphic organizers are included at the back of this book so that you can copy them as often as needed.

Since the same essential research strategies apply to every subject area, the lessons do not differentiate among science, math, social studies, and English. When appropriate, however, sample research topics are given for each subject area. You may want to direct your students to choose the most subject-specific topic in the list, or you may allow them to choose any topic from the list. Also, subject-specific readings are grouped at the back of the book, following the lessons. Students can use these readings to practice and develop the skills they have learned in the lessons.

TO THE STUDENT

Imagine this scenario. A few years ago, you bought a car—and it turned out to be a complete lemon. Nothing about it ever worked properly. You spent more time standing at the side of the road waiting for a tow truck than you spent actually driving the car. Your mechanic saw more of you than anyone else.

Finally, a miracle happened. Someone rear-ended your car, and the insurance company is giving you money to get a new one. This time, you're going to make sure you avoid the lemons. You're going to get a car that works.

First, you decide what you really want in a car in terms of size, features, and so forth. Next, you read car magazines to find out which cars have the features you want. You talk to people, asking them about their cars. What car do they have? What do they like about it? What don't they like? Then you read consumer reports to find out what test drivers say about different cars. You do Internet searches to see what people who own certain cars have to say. Then you organize all the information you've gotten. By the time you're done, you know exactly which cars to avoid, and which ones to consider.

In fact, you do research on cars following a step-by-step process—almost the same process you would use for any research project. You start with a topic you need to research, find information about the topic, evaluate the information, organize it, and come to a conclusion.

The lessons in this book will give you the tools you need to go through that process and complete a research project for any subject area. You have probably used some of these tools before. But now you will learn how to combine them to make the research process easier. You will see how organizing your work before you get started will save you time as you go on, and will keep you on track each step of the way.

Of course, everyone has his or her own approach to doing research. As you go through the lessons in this book, see which strategies work best for you. Adapt the graphic organizers to fit your needs. In the end, you will have a customized approach to completing the organization, research, documentation, and writing that go into a good research project.

PART I
The Research Topic

LESSON 1
Getting Organized

When you are assigned a research paper, it can seem fairly simple: do some research, then write a paper. If the due date for the paper is weeks away, it can be tempting to wait until nearer the date before getting started.

However, you should keep in mind that a research project calls for many different steps. If you try to squeeze them all in at the end, the quality of your work will suffer. It takes time to collect resources and do the research. For a standard research paper, you should give yourself a month.

To make sure you use your time well, you should organize your work in advance. Start by identifying all the steps in the process. Then set a schedule for completing them.

Identify the Steps

Although each research project is unique in some ways, all projects call for many of the same steps.
1. Choose a topic.
2. Find resources (books, magazines, electronic media, and so on) with information on your topic.
3. Gather information from your resources, taking detailed notes to keep track of which information came from each source.
4. Organize your notes in preparation for writing.
5. Write the paper.

Set a Schedule

The time each step will take varies widely. For example, if you already know a lot about the subject, choosing a topic and finding resources may not take very long. But if the whole subject is unfamiliar, you may have to do a lot of reading before you can decide what to write about. Also, the time you are given will vary. If you have two weeks to do a project, you will need to spend less time on each step than if you have a month.

Try breaking the time down by percentages. Assign a certain percentage of the total time to each part of the process. That way you can make a reasonable schedule based on your total time.

Getting Organized *(continued)*

Here are some average percentages for each step. Remember, these are only averages. You may need to spend more time on one step and less on another. Use these as a starting point to work out your schedule.

Planning—5%

Choosing a topic—10%

Finding a focus—20%

Gathering information—25%

Preparing to write—10%

Writing and revising—30%

Model
To organize your time, you can use a graphic organizer like this one. Figure out the total amount of time you have available, and about how much time you'll need for each step. Then set deadlines for each step.

Assignment date: _____

Due date: _____

Step-by-step research and writing	% of time	date you will finish
Step 1: Planning the process	5%	10/3
Step 2: Choosing a topic	10%	10/6
Step 3: Finding the focus for your topic	20%	10/12
Step 4: Gathering information	25%	10/19
Step 5: Preparing to write	10%	10/22
Step 6: Writing and revising	30%	10/31

In this example, the student has been given a total of one month for research. About 70 percent of the time has been set aside for preparation and research. The remaining time—30 percent—has been set aside for writing.

Application
To practice organizing your time for the research paper, imagine that you have been given a month for a project about inventions. Start by asking yourself, "What do I already know about inventions? What kind of inventions would I like to know more about?"

Getting Organized *(continued)*

Based on your answers to these questions, complete the graphic organizer below. Use today's date as the assignment date. Use a date one month from today as the due date. Then set appropriate deadlines for completing each step.

Assignment date: _____

Due date: _____

Step-by-step research and writing	% of time	date you will finish
Step 1: Planning the process	5%	
Step 2: Choosing a topic	10%	
Step 3: Finding the focus for your topic	20%	
Step 4: Gathering information	25%	
Step 5: Preparing to write	10%	
Step 6: Writing and revising	30%	

Customizing Some people work best if every single step in the process is written out. Checking off steps as they are completed really helps these people stay on track. If that's the way you tend to work, keep that in mind as you learn more about the steps in the research process. You can then customize your schedule by including as many smaller steps as you like. Your list of steps might look more like this:

1. Choose a topic.
2. Use encyclopedias to get background information.
3. Identify the main concepts in the topic.
4. Find resources with information on the topic.
5. Gather information from resources, taking detailed notes to keep track of which information came from each source.
6. Evaluate the resources for reliability, accuracy, bias, and so on.
7. Organize the notes in preparation for writing.
8. Prepare an outline.
9. Write a first draft.
10. Revise and edit the first draft to create a final draft.
11. Prepare the bibliography.

Getting Organized *(continued)*

Some people find grouping small steps together works best for them. If that's the best approach for you, your list of steps might look like this:

1. Prepare
2. Research
3. Write and revise

There is no one "right" way to organize your time. Use the graphic organizer as a starting point. Then add or delete steps to make the schedule fit your needs.

LESSON 2
Choosing a Topic

This probably seems like the easiest part of the research process. Usually, your teacher gives you a general topic. In that case, you assume, you will write about whatever is assigned. The problem here is that the general topic is usually just that—very general. It might be "The Novels of Charles Dickens," or "The History of Writing," or "The Civil War." You couldn't possibly cover any of these topics; they're just too big. You need to choose a smaller part of the general topic to write about.

It's also important to choose a topic that interests you. You're going to spend a lot of time researching and writing about it; why put all that energy into something you don't care about? And, of course, if you're interested in the topic, your interest will show. You'll write a better paper—and get a better grade.

Background Information

Your first step should be to do some background reading to find out a little about the general topic. Textbooks and encyclopedias (both print and CD-ROM) are good places to start. They have a little information about a lot of subjects, and that's all you want at this stage. Read what they have to say about the general topic.

As you read, keep a notebook handy. You may get ideas for possible topics. Write these ideas down. You should also write down any questions you find yourself wondering about as you read. If something makes you curious, it may be a good research topic.

Model

This excerpt is an encyclopedia entry about Charles Dickens. Read the entry. Then see the notes and questions one student jotted down while reading the article.

> Dickens, Charles (1812–1870) Prolific and popular English novelist known for masterful storytelling, sharp social criticism, and accurate observations of people and places. Dickens wrote some 20 books, many of which appeared in monthly installments in magazines. They often included parallel plots, with many different stories running at the same time. At the end of

(continued)

the book, all the separate stories are connected and resolved.

Dickens spent much of his childhood in the English county of Kent. In 1824, when Dickens was 11, his father was sent to prison for debt. Young Charles was forced to support himself. He lived in a rented room and worked in a factory.

Although this period lasted only a few months, it made a lasting impression. Dickens's father became the model for Mr. Micawber in *David Copperfield* (1849–50). Micawber is a great optimist who cannot manage money and is constantly running up debts. Life in a debtor's prison was described in *Our Mutual Friend* (1864–65). Dickens's own experience in the factory was described in *David Copperfield*. A boy he met in the factory became the model for the Artful Dodger in *Oliver Twist* (1838–39).

Notes and Questions

- What kind of "social criticism" did he write?

- Wow—I can't imagine having to work in a factory at the age of 11. I wonder what that was like.

- It sounds like Dickens used real people for some of his characters, or at least bits of their lives. I wonder if he did that with other characters, too.

- There's a big range of dates on the books named here. One was published in 1838–39, one in 1849–50, one in 1864–65. I wonder when his first book was published. If he wrote for so many years, I'll bet his style really changed over time.

From these notes, the student could come up with several possible topics: "Social Criticism in the Novels of Charles Dickens," "Charles Dickens, Child Factory Worker," "Real People as Dickens Characters," "Changes in Dickens's Writing over Time." Any one of these would be a more manageable topic than "The Novels of Charles Dickens."

Application   This excerpt is part of an encyclopedia entry on the history of writing. As you read it, make notes about possible research topics.

The History of Writing

Writing as a means of communication is almost as old as civilization itself. All the earliest known civilizations developed systems of writing.

The earliest known writing system developed around 3300 B.C.E. in Sumeria, between the Tigris and Euphrates rivers. Sumerian scribes used cut reeds

(continued)

Choosing a Topic *(continued)*

to press marks into damp clay. When the clay hardened, the marks were preserved. This writing has been given the name *cuneiform*, which means "wedge-shaped," because the reeds made wedge-shaped marks.

About 200 years later, around 3100 B.C.E., hieroglyphic writing developed in Egypt. This system used pictorial symbols to represent both words and sounds. Carved into stone and painted on tomb walls, these symbols were preserved for centuries after their meanings had been forgotten. The first clue to this writing system came in 1799, when the Rosetta Stone was found in Egypt. This stone tablet contained writing in several different scripts. For years, scholars worked to decode the writing on the stone. Finally, in 1823, Jean-François Champollion, a French Egyptologist, deciphered the stone. The meaning of hieroglyphics could again be understood.

Possible Research Topics

_____

_____

_____

_____

_____

_____

_____

_____

_____

_____

_____

_____

LESSON 3
Finding a Focus

In Lesson 2, you learned how to find an interesting research topic. The next step is to narrow that topic. Which specific aspect of the topic are you going to cover?

For example, look back at the third suggested Dickens topic on page 7, "Real People as Dickens Characters." The topic sounds interesting. We know that Dickens based some of his characters on real people. But we also know that he wrote about twenty books, and that some of his books told a lot of different stories. That probably means Dickens created hundreds and hundreds of characters. Trying to find out which of them were based on real people would take a lot of work.

Narrowing the Scope

You can narrow the scope of a topic in several different ways: people, classification, time, location, reason, method, and so forth. And you can combine two or more of these approaches for an even narrower focus.

- **People.** Focus on one individual, or a specific group of people. (Who?)

- **Classification.** Focus on one aspect of the issue, one style of music, genre of painting, species of animal, and so forth. (What?)

- **Time.** Focus on a specific era, period, or set of years. (When?)

- **Location.** Focus on one specific place or region, rather than an entire country, or the whole world. (Where?)

- **Reason.** Examine a reason or reasons behind your topic. (Why?)

- **Method.** Focus on one strategy, tactic, action, interpretation, or function. (How?)

Six Basic Questions

Try asking the six basic questions about your topic: who? what? when? where? why? how?

- Who was involved, or affected? One particular individual? A group of people—women, teenagers, the homeless, migrant farm workers? Does your topic affect animals, or involve plants? To whom is it important?

Finding a Focus *(continued)*

- What was involved? What happened? What are the issues? What different aspects does one issue have? What specific aspect do I want to cover? What species/genres/styles/media can I choose from? What specific type will I research?

- When did an issue become important? What was the time span for an event—a day, a week, the 1970s, the eighteenth century? If it covered a long time span, do you want to concentrate on a specific part of that time?

- Where did an event take place? Where did an individual live? Where does a condition apply—globally, or locally? In one town, a whole state, a region, country, continent? If it applies to a wide area, is there a specific part of that area you can focus on?

- Why is it important? Why did it happen?

- How does it work? How was it discovered? How can it be fixed, addressed, analyzed?

Model This student was assigned the general topic "Environmental Issues." She chose "Invasive Species" as her specific topic. To narrow the topic further, she asked herself these questions:

- Who is working on the problem?

- What level of classification do I want to research—all invasive species, a class of organisms (e.g., mammals, reptiles, birds), or a smaller group—an order, family, genus, or species?

- What time period will I cover?

- Where do I want to cover—the entire United States, or a region?

- Why are invasive species a problem?

- How do invasive species spread? How can the spread be stopped?

Based on her answers, the student decided to narrow the topic in terms of location, classification, and period. For a location she chose the Great Lakes region. For classification she chose one species, the zebra mussel. For period she chose the last twenty years. Her focused topic: "Zebra Mussels in the Great Lakes Since 1980."

The who, why, and how questions would form the body of her paper. She could research what scientists are working on concerning the issue of zebra mussels invading the Great Lakes, why it is a problem, how it occurred, and how it can be stopped.

Finding a Focus *(continued)*

To make her research easier, she turned her topic into a question: "How do zebra mussels in the Great Lakes region spread, and how can they be stopped?"

Application   Choose one of the research topics below. Use the six basic questions—who, what, when, where, why, how—to narrow and focus the topic. Then write your focused topic as a question.

The Rain Forest

Ancient Rome

The Printing Press

Number Systems

Topic: _____

Who? _____

What? _____

When? _____

Where? _____

Why? _____

How? _____

Focused topic: _____?

PART II
The Research Process

LESSON 4
Identify the Key Concepts

The first step in the research process is to identify the key concepts in the topic. You may wonder, "Why should I identify the concepts now? Isn't that what I'll be doing as I research?" Yes, you will. But identifying some of the main ideas now will help you focus your research. You will be able to work more efficiently.

Also, identifying important concepts will make searching on the computer easier. You will be using electronic resources such as on-line library catalogs and periodical indexes. You can use the concepts you identify as keywords in electronic searches.

One way to identify key terms is by brainstorming. Write down anything that comes into your head when you think about your topic. Ask the six basic questions again, but this time about your focused topic.

Use a brainstorming web to organize your ideas. Then you can look at the web to see which ideas seem most important.

Model

To use a brainstorming web, write your topic in the center circle. Write related ideas in the smaller circles. Ideas can include things you know about the topic and questions you would like to know more about.

Identify the Key Concepts *(continued)*

Here is one student's brainstorming web on the topic "How did Jean-François Champollion come to decipher the Rosetta Stone?"

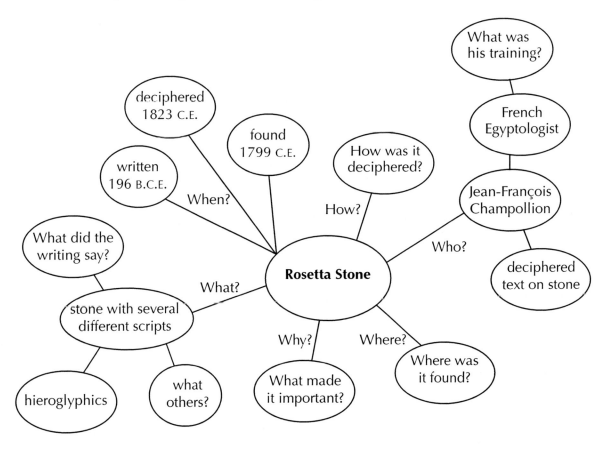

Based on the web, here are some possible key concepts for this topic.

Key Concepts

Rosetta Stone

    Stone with several different scripts

    What scripts were on the stone?

    What did the writing say?

    Why was the stone important?

How was it deciphered?

Jean-François Champollion

    French Egyptologist

Identify the Key Concepts *(continued)*

Application Use the brainstorming web to identify key concepts for the research question. Add more lines and circles if you need them. Then list the key concepts below the web.

Research Question: "What are the pros and cons of homework?"

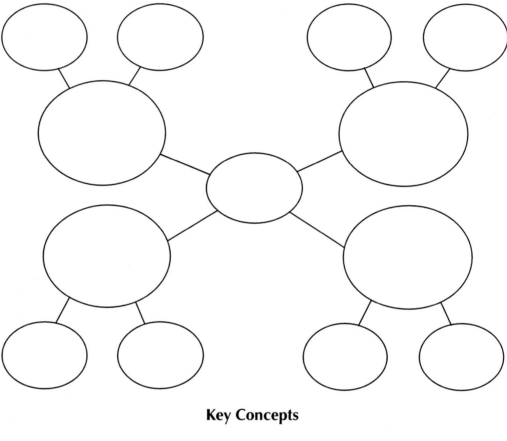

Key Concepts

_____

_____

_____

_____

_____

_____

_____

_____

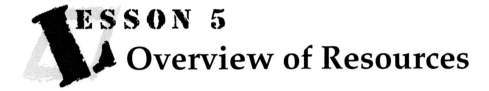

ESSON 5
Overview of Resources

Types of Resources

Finally, you've finished all the preparation for your research project. You've worked out when you need to have each step done, you've found a focused topic, and you've identified the main concepts. You're ready to start the actual research.

The only trouble is—where do you start? There's a lot of information out there, in a lot of different forms. Which resources have the best information?

For most research projects, you will need several different kinds of information. Some resources can give you general background information. These are generally reference books.

Some can provide very detailed information about a narrow subject. These include books on specific topics and articles in magazines and newspapers.

And, of course, there's the Internet. You can find references, such as dictionaries, here, as well as books, journal articles, and newspapers.

It's usually most helpful to start with the general sources. Once you have the background information, you can move to more specific sources. Here are some of the most useful printed resources.

Reference Materials

Reference books are useful places to start your research. They are not designed to be read all the way through, but to be checked quickly. Most reference books include indexes or tables of contents to help you find information. In some, all the information is in alphabetical order. Some are available on CD-ROM or on-line. This makes it easy to search for key terms.

Reference books include almanacs, atlases, dictionaries, encyclopedias, and so forth. Ask the reference librarian for more information about these resources.

Books

Books on a specific subject are the next stop for research. This is where you will find the established knowledge about a topic. Books offer in-depth coverage of a subject. Use the library catalog and your keywords to find books on your topic.

Periodical Articles

Periodicals are resources that are published at regular intervals (daily, weekly, etc.). They include newspapers and magazines. Because of their schedule, periodicals can include current information on a subject. They cover events that are too new to be treated in books. Use a periodical index, either on the computer or in print form, to locate periodical articles for your topic.

The Internet

The Internet can give you access to all sorts of information. But "all sorts" can include things that are wrong as well as things that are right. Remember, anyone can post anything on the Web.

However, many reference materials are now available on-line. This makes searching these materials much easier. Many sites are hosted by government bodies, educational institutions, or other reliable organizations. Most newspapers now have on-line versions. This makes it easy to get information about very recent events. These sites are all very useful for doing research.

When you use the Internet for research, it's important to keep a few things in mind:

- Anyone can create a web site; just because it's on the Web doesn't mean it's true.
- Search engines can turn up thousands of hits. It's important to narrow your search by using search terms.
- You need to evaluate web sites before you rely on the information.
- Different search engines use different approaches. The same search terms will give different results.
- Not everything is available on-line.

How to Get Started

1. Get background information from a general reference source.
2. Use the library catalog to find books on your topic.
3. Use a periodical index to find articles on your topic.
4. If you need to know about government organizations, museums, universities, or other public bodies, use a search engine to find information on the Internet.

Overview of Resources *(continued)*

Application Choose one of the research topics below. Think about the resources you would need to research this topic. Then write out a plan for the research. Name the topic you chose, which type of resources you would start with, which you would check second, and so forth.

- The Cherokee Trail of Tears: 1838–1839
- Mass Media: Images of Women in Advertising
- Francis Crick and Jim Watson: Discovering the Double Helix of DNA
- Famous Mathematicians of the Twentieth Century

Research Topic: _____

My Research Plan

1. Background information: _____
2. Subject-specific information: _____
3. Supporting information: _____
4. Other: _____

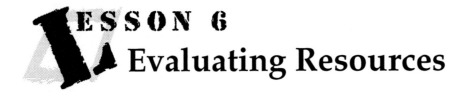

ESSON 6
Evaluating Resources

Evaluating Resources

All resources are not equal. Some offer objective, accurate information. Others are biased and inaccurate. Some might be good for one type of project but not for another.

Before you read a resource, you should evaluate its usefulness. If it is inaccurate or out of date, you shouldn't use the information. If the information just isn't relevant for your topic, you'll be wasting your time if you read it.

In a lot of ways, evaluating sources is like detective work. You have to decide what clues to search for, and what to accept. There are certain basic things to check: relevance, credibility, objectivity, accuracy and scope, and support.

These criteria can be used for all resources. However, it is especially important to evaluate Internet resources. Anyone can put anything up on the Internet. There is no quality control. Because of this, the next lesson will give some Internet-specific suggestions.

Relevance

Whether the resource is a journal article or a web page, it is designed for a certain audience. This can affect its appropriateness for your topic. If your topic is "Deforestation in the Amazon: Causes and Consequences," a web page about one person's trip to Brazil won't help you.

Relevance is also affected by timeliness. In some fields information goes out of date quickly. In other fields material stays relevant longer. If your topic is Victorian novels, "timely" could mean "written any time since the mid-1900s." If your topic is technology, "timely" means "within the last three months." To evaluate relevance, ask questions like these:

- Who is the intended audience—experts in the field? a general audience?
- Is the vocabulary simple or technical?
- Is the source too elementary, too specialized, too general, or just right for your needs?

Evaluating Resources *(continued)*

- When was the source published? Based on your topic, is the material current and timely?

Credibility

The ideal resource comes from a source you can trust. But how can you tell which ones are credible? You need to know information about the author and the publisher. To evaluate credibility, ask questions like these:

- Who is the author?
- Are the author's qualifications, experience, and/or institutional affiliation given? If so, are they in a field relevant to the information? Is the person respected in the field?
- On a web site, does the author provide contact information (e-mail or snail mail address, phone number)?
- Who published or produced the resource?
- Is the publisher a university press, a government body, a company, an individual?
- What bias or purpose might the publisher have?

Objectivity

Objective resources give fair, balanced coverage of a subject. They try to show all sides of an issue. Some resources present opinions as if they were facts. Some have a purpose besides just sharing information: They may be trying to sell you something or convince you of something. In doing research, it is important to know if information is fact or opinion, biased or objective. For example, if a car manufacturer produces a site about its newest model, you probably won't find negative comments about the car. The publisher is biased in favor of the car.

To evaluate objectivity, ask questions like these:

- Why was this resource made? to inform? to persuade? to present opinions? to report research? to sell a product?
- Is the tone objective (calm, reasonable) or emotional (too enthusiastic, too critical)?
- Does the information seem valid and well researched, or questionable and unsupported by evidence?
- Is a point of view being promoted? Does the author or publisher have some interest (financial, political, and so forth) in this point of view?
- Are opposing viewpoints presented accurately, or treated as crazy?

Evaluating Resources *(continued)*

Accuracy and Scope

To be useful, a source needs to have accurate information. It also needs to address enough of your topic for your purposes. To evaluate accuracy and scope, ask questions like these:

- Is the coverage comprehensive? Are there aspects of the topic that it doesn't cover?
- Is the information useful for my topic?
- Does it update other sources I have read, or add new information?
- Does it give the whole story, or does it leave out important facts or alternatives?
- Does the content agree with other sources I have read, or does it seem to contradict them? (If two sources don't agree, it's hard to tell which one is right. Check more sources before making up your mind.)
- Does the content agree with what I already know about the topic? (If a source is wrong about something you already know, it may be wrong in other areas, too.)
- Do the author's claims seem likely, or far-fetched? Do they make sense? (If they're hard to believe, look for more evidence before you accept them.)
- Is the material logical and sensible?

Support

One way to tell fact from opinion is by the support provided. If material is well-researched and based on established facts, the author will usually tell you so. Footnotes and references will point you to other sources with those facts. If it is based on the author's opinion, there probably won't be references to other sources. If the information sounds too good to be true, it probably isn't true. Never use information you cannot verify.

To evaluate support, ask questions like these:

- Where did the information in the source come from? Are there footnotes, bibliographies, or lists of references so that I can confirm statistics or factual information?
- Does the author make sweeping generalizations that oversimplify things?
- Does the author give evidence to support conclusions?

Evaluating Resources *(continued)*

Application   You can use a checklist like this one to evaluate resources. You should be able to answer "Yes" to most questions.

Materials Evaluation Checklist

1. Is the date of the source current enough for my topic? Yes ___ No ___

2. Is the material relevant to my topic? Yes ___ No ___

3. Is the author a credible source, with authority and expertise in the field?
   Yes ___ No ___

4. Is the publisher a reliable, unbiased source of material on this topic?
   Yes ___ No ___

5. Is evidence provided to support all statements? Yes ___ No ___

6. Is the coverage suitable for my topic? Yes ___ No ___

7. Does the information agree with what I already know about the subject?
   Yes ___ No ___

8. Does the information make sense? Yes ___ No ___

9. Is the language reasonable and objective? Yes ___ No ___

LESSON 7
Evaluating Internet Sources

Internet Sources

To evaluate an Internet source, start by asking the same questions you would ask about a book or an article. You need to know the author, the sponsoring organization, any bias, and so forth. But because material on the Internet has no quality control, you'll need to know more.

Authorship

The first thing you need to know is the type of site you are looking at. If the site is run by a government agency, you can be fairly sure the material has been checked for accuracy. If the site is a commercial one, the purpose of the site is probably to sell you something. If it is a personal web page, you should be careful about how you use the information. Personal web pages usually aren't good sources for facts.

You can often tell what kind of site it is by looking at the extension on the URL.

Common Web Site Extensions

.biz	commercial business	.museum	accredited museums
.com	commercial site	.mil	military agency
.edu	educational institution (U.S.)	.name	individual
.gov	government agency	.net	internet service provider
.info	unrestricted—can be anyone	.org	nonprofit organization

Some URLs have a two-letter code at the end, such as .ie or .ch. These are country codes (.ie—Ireland; .ch—Switzerland). However, the country code doesn't guarantee that the site is based in that country. Some URLs include a tilde (~). This often means that the site is a personal web page.

Content-Area Research Strategies

Evaluating Internet Sources *(continued)*

Access

- Do users need to register a name and password to use the site?
- Do users need to pay to use the site?
- How reliable are the links? Do many of them lead to dead ends or sites that have moved?
- Do links only lead to other pages on the same site, or do they lead to other sites?
- How easy is navigation within the site? How many links does it take to get to the information?
- Can the site be "viewed" by all web browsers?
- Is response time fast?
- Is a text-only version available?
- Can I rely on the site staying up?
- Will the site continue to be maintained and updated?
- Is there a link to a search engine or is a search engine embedded in the web site?

Coverage

- Is the web site linked to a print or CD-ROM version?
- Is the information on the web site the same as the print version? (Some newspapers have some, but not all, information in their on-line versions.)

Model

For a report on volcanoes, you have found this site:

http://vulcan.wr.usgs.gov/

When you check the site, you find that it is run by the U.S. Geological Survey. The home page includes the name of the person you should contact if you have any questions, as well as the date of the most recent update. It also includes information about The USGS Volcano Hazards Program (VHP) and U.S. Volcano Observatories. The links on the home page are well organized and clearly presented. A search engine is embedded in the site.

Based on the evaluation criteria, this is probably a reliable web site.

Evaluating Internet Sources *(continued)*

Application   You are preparing a report on the *Exxon Valdez* oil spill. A search engine has given you the following list of web sites. You don't have time to go to all the sites to evaluate them. Based on the URLs and the search engine's summary, which ones will you visit? Put a check mark beside each site that you think might be worthwhile. Put an x beside any site you don't think is worth visiting. Put a question mark beside any site that you can't evaluate with this information.

___ 1. http://www.oilspillcommission.gov

The text of the final report of the Alaska Oil Spill Commission, published February 1990 by the State of Alaska.

___ 2. http://www.fakr.noaa.gov/oil/default.htm

National Oceanic and Atmospheric Administration (NOAA) site evaluating the 1989 *Exxon Valdez* oil spill, including the environmental impact of the 10.8 million gallons of oil released in the spill.

___ 3. http://www.friendsofthecoast.org

Friends of the Coast is an environmental watchdog group pledged to the restoration of the Kenai Peninsula. Local wildlife is still severely affected by the record-breaking spill, the biggest the world has ever seen. Much more restoration work is needed.

___ 4. http://www.what~spill.name

The *Exxon Valdez* oil spill never happened. The whole thing was dreamed up by environmentalists to give the oil industry a bad name.

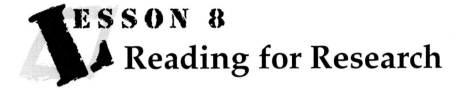

LESSON 8
Reading for Research

Before You Read

Before you start reading books and articles that focus on your topic, get a general idea of the topic. Read overviews in reference sources like encyclopedias. This will give you the grounding you need to get started.

Next, get an overview of the books you have chosen. Use the techniques of scanning and skimming to analyze them quickly. Do this for all your chosen sources before you start reading for content. This will help you see how your sources fit together.

Scanning

Scanning is a way to get a general impression of a book's contents. It makes you familiar with the book's basic structure.

1. Look carefully at the book's complete title. Sometimes the main title doesn't give as much information as the subtitle.

2. Read through the preface, foreword, and introduction. This should tell you the author's purpose in writing the book. You should also learn how the subject will be approached and what material will be covered.

3. Scan the table of contents. Is your topic covered in enough depth to be useful?

4. Look at the index. Which entries have the most page numbers listed? These are the subjects that the book focuses on. If your topic is just a small part of the book's subject, the index entries can take you straight to the most relevant sections.

5. Scan the book, reading subheads in each chapter, looking at graphics (photos, maps, illustrations, and so forth), and reading captions. Charts and figures often summarize the major ideas and facts of a chapter.

6. Ask yourself: "Based on my background knowledge, does this book have enough relevant information to be useful?"

Application This excerpt is about Egyptian art. Don't read the excerpt yet. Scan it by reading the title, subheads, and captions. Look at the illustration.

Egyptian Painting

Much of what we know about ancient Egyptians comes from their art. The walls of tombs were decorated with scenes of everyday life. We see pictures of people working in the fields, baking, fishing, boating, playing, and relaxing with family and friends.

Angles in Egyptian Art

If you have seen reproductions of Egyptian paintings, you have probably noticed that people are shown at a strange angle. Their heads are always shown in profile, their shoulders face forward, and their chests, waists, and legs are in profile. If you try to stand in this position, you will realize that Egyptian artists weren't painting people the way they really looked. But it's obvious that these ancient artists were able to draw very well. Why did they draw people in a way that seems so strange to us?

Purpose of Egyptian Art

Our art would seem just as odd to the ancient Egyptians as theirs seems to us. That's because artists today and in ancient Egypt had very different purposes in mind. Tomb paintings show ideal versions of people—the way people wanted to look in their

(continued)

Purpose of Egyptian Art (continued)

new eternal life. Physical problems were rarely shown. Egyptian artists even avoided showing any emotion on the faces of their paintings.

Ancient Egyptian artists were not trying to draw what they saw but what they knew was there. When they drew figures on the walls of tombs, they expected their drawings to come to life in the Afterlife. It was important to show every part of the body as clearly as possible. If an arm or a leg in tomb artwork could not be seen clearly, the person might not be able to use that arm or leg in the Afterlife.

Rules of Drawing

To make sure tomb paintings were as complete and correct as possible, rules for art developed. In a group of people, an important person would be drawn much larger than other people. Heads were shown in profile, but the eyes looked as if they were seen from the front. The shoulders and chest were seen from the front. The waist and legs were in profile. Both arms were clearly shown, as well as the fingers on each hand. The left leg was usually in front of the right one, and as much as possible was shown of both legs.

Adapted from *Hands-on Culture of Ancient Egypt* by Kate O'Halloran. © 1997 by J. Weston Walch, Publisher.

Based on your scan of the article, write what you think it is about.

_____

Skimming

Skimming builds on the information you found through scanning. It helps you identify the book's purpose and main ideas. When you skim, you don't need to read every word. Just read enough to get a general idea of the material. You will be reading the relevant material more closely later.

1. If the first chapter is an overview of the subject, read through it quickly.

2. Read the first and last sections of each chapter. The first section usually explains what the author plans to cover in that chapter. The last section usually summarizes the chapter and gives the author's conclusions. Make a note of any sections that seem particularly useful. You can go back and read them more carefully later.

3. If there is a summary chapter at the end of the book, read through it.

Reading for Research *(continued)*

Application

Look at the article on pages 28–29 again. This time, skim it for information. Read the first and last paragraphs of the article. Read the first and last sentences of the other paragraphs. Based on this, write what you think the main points of the article are.

_____

_____

As You Read   Scanning and skimming have given you an overview of the book. You have also identified the parts that address your topic. The next step calls for careful reading of the relevant sections. If you come across unfamiliar words, note them. Look them up in a dictionary to be sure you understand them. Remind yourself of your research question. As you read, you should be looking for information that will help you answer that question. Later lessons will explain how to record the details of the book for your bibliography, and how to take notes.

If you come to difficult passages, read more slowly. Stop and reread any parts that are not clear.

As you read, look for the author's major points and ideas. Try to distinguish fact from opinion. What is the writer's argument? What is the writer's conclusion?

At the same time, keep evaluating the material. Use the same criteria you used to evaluate resources in advance. Is the material accurate, comprehensive, unbiased, timely? Are assertions and conclusions well supported by the evidence? How does it fit in with what you already know?

Reading Articles

Articles from magazines and newspapers can be approached in much the same way. Of course, since they are shorter, the process is easier. These articles can usually be divided into three types. Each type has a different purpose, and the information in them is arranged differently. If you can tell which type an article falls into, you can quickly find the information you need.

Reading for Research *(continued)*

News

These articles are the meat of most newspapers. In a news article, the most important information is presented first. The rest of the article adds detail to the key points.

Opinion

The purpose of these pieces is to present a point of view. This viewpoint is usually presented in the introduction, and restated in the summary. The rest of the article consists of arguments that support the writer's opinion.

Features

Feature articles are designed to provide background about a subject. Here, the most important information is in the body of the article.

Content-Area Research Strategies

LESSON 9
Recording Bibliographic Information

In the lesson on evaluating resources, we talked about the importance of showing evidence for facts and conclusions. That holds true for a research paper, too. You need to be able to back up your statements by referring to the sources you consulted. When you finish writing your paper, you will need to prepare a bibliography. This is a listing of all the sources you used, with details that would let a reader find each source.

To prepare a bibliography, you will need to keep track of your sources. It's very easy to lose track of your sources. The best way to avoid this is to record the information for each source as soon as you decide to use that source.

Information Needed for Different Sources

Of course, different types of sources call for different details. The left-hand column below explains the details required for the most common types of resources. The right-hand column gives an example of each type.

Book

Author (authors, if more than one):	Hannah Holmes
Title (underlined)	The Secret Life of Dust: From the Cosmos to the Kitchen Counter, the Big Consequences of Little Things
Place of Publication:	New York
Publisher:	John Wiley & Sons, Inc.
Copyright date:	2001

Encyclopedia

Author (if given):	Peter Goodman
"Title of article" (in quotation marks):	"The Art of Negotiation"
Name of encyclopedia (underlined):	Encyclopedia Hibernica
Edition (year):	2002
Volume number:	1

Recording Bibliographic Information *(continued)*

Magazine, Newspaper, or Journal Article

Author of article: | Laura Dabundo

"Title of article" (in quotation marks) | "'The Voice of the Mute': Wordsworth and the Ideology of Romantic Silences."

Name of magazine (underlined) | Christianity and Literature

Volume number: | 43:1

Date: | 1995

Pages: | 21–35

Video or Film

Title (underlined): | Do the Right Thing

Director: | Spike Lee

Distributor: | Forty Acres and a Mule Filmworks

Year released: | 1989

Television Program

"Episode title" (in quotation marks): | "Provenance"

Show title (underlined): | The X-Files

Producer: | Fox. WXIA, Atlanta

Air date: | 3 March 2002

Internet

Author's name (if available): | William J. Duiker

Title of document: | "Ho Chi Minh"

Source organization (if available): | Encarta Online Encyclopedia. Microsoft Corporation.

<URL> (between angle brackets): | <http://encarta.msn.com>

Date accessed: | 26 Sept. 2001

LESSON 10
Preparing Bibliography Cards

The notetaking system we will be using calls for two sets of 3×5 index cards. One set of cards is for your bibliographic information. The other set is for your notes. Each source is given an identifying number, starting with "1."

This system means you only need to record the information for each source once. On a 3×5 index card, write the bibliographic details and the identifying number, such as "Source 1." As you take notes on your reading, you can identify the source by number. There is no need to write all the information out each time. When you write notes from that source, you just need to indicate the identifying number.

To prepare bibliography cards, follow these steps.

1. Write one card for each source.

2. Starting with the number "1," number each source. Write the source number in the upper right-hand corner of the card.

3. Below the source number, write the source type.

4. List the required information on each card. Use the checklist from Lesson 9 for details.

Model

Here is a bibliography card for a book.

source number

Author: John Haywood   Source #3

Title: <u>The Encyclopedic Dictionary</u>   Type: Encyclopedia
<u>of American History</u> (3rd ed.)

required information—

Place of publication: Guilford, CT

Publisher: Dushkin Publishing Group

Copyright date: 1986

Preparing Bibliography Cards *(continued)*

Application   Each of these paragraphs includes the required bibliographic information for one source. Use the information to prepare a bibliography card for each source.

Bibliography Card 1

I used an article I found in <u>Time</u> magazine. It was written by Lisa Beyer. The article was about causes of anger; it was called "Roots of Rage." The issue of the magazine was October 1, 2001. The article started on page 40 and finished on page 42.

35

Preparing Bibliography Cards *(continued)*

Bibliography Card 2

For background material, I used the <u>Encyclopedia of North American Indians</u>. It was published in New York by Marshall Cavendish. This edition is from 1997. The specific article I found was written by T. Midge. It was called "Powwows."

LESSON 11
Taking Notes

The main purpose of taking notes is to get information that you can use for a clear, logical paper. As you read, look for facts or ideas that will help you do this. Review the list of main concepts and keywords you prepared at the start of the research process. Look for information that addresses those concepts. Include facts that fill in the blanks, information that answers questions, or ideas that support your own ideas.

Identify the Main Idea

The best way to take notes is to look at whole paragraphs, not just sentences. Don't take any notes until you have read the whole paragraph. Be sure you understand everything you have read. If anything is unclear, reread it.

Then look for the main idea in the paragraph. Don't be distracted by details or unrelated information. Ask, "What one idea is the author trying to express in this paragraph?"

Once you have identified the main idea, check its relevance to your topic. If it doesn't address your topic at all, don't take notes on it. Taking notes you know you can't use just makes the process longer.

If the main idea does address your topic, make a note of it. Use your own words to take notes. Try to write down only the main idea, not the details. Lesson 12 will explain how to record the information on the cards.

Model

This excerpt comes from a discussion of democracy in ancient Greece. The research topic is "Democracy in Ancient Athens: Rule of All the People, or Some of the People?"

The Beginnings of Democracy

Until about 508 B.C.E., many Greek city-states were ruled by one man who had complete control. Then an Athenian named Cleisthenes suggested a new system of government. This new system would involve a lot more people in governing the city. The Greek word for people was *demos*, and the word for government was *kratos*. These words were eventually combined to give a name to the new system: *demokratia*—democracy. It means "government by the people."

(continued)

Taking Notes *(continued)*

The Beginnings of Democracy (continued)

This new system involved all the citizens of Athens in government. The laws of Athens were made by the Assembly. This consisted of any citizens of Athens who chose to take part. The Assembly met about every ten days. At least 6,000 citizens had to be present to hold a meeting of the Assembly. If too few citizens came, special police were sent out to bring more citizens to the meeting. These meetings began early in the morning and could go on until dark. The Assembly decided on laws and public policies such as taxes and building programs.

Adapted from *Hands-on Culture of Ancient Greece and Rome* by Kate O'Halloran. © 1998 by J. Weston Walch, Publisher.

Main idea, paragraph 1: Democracy, new system of "government by the people," developed in Athens around 508 B.C.E.

Main idea, paragraph 2: All citizens of Athens were involved in the government as part of the Assembly, which decided on laws, public policies.

These paragraphs also include a lot of interesting details: before democracy city-states had one all-powerful ruler; the new system was suggested by a man named Cleisthenes; the Greek word for people is *demos*; and so forth. But these are just details, not the main idea.

Now we need to look at the research topic: "Democracy in Ancient Athens: Rule of All the People, or Some of the People?" Are these ideas relevant to the topic? Yes, they are. The first paragraph gives background information about the history of democracy and explains the meaning of the word. The second paragraph describes how Athenian citizens were involved in government.

Application

Here are the next two paragraphs in the same excerpt. Read each paragraph carefully. Make sure you understand everything it is saying. Then, on the lines below, write the main idea of each paragraph. Say whether or not you think this idea is relevant to the topic "Democracy in Ancient Athens: Rule of All the People, or Some of the People?"

Taking Notes *(continued)*

Of course, it's important to remember that not all people in Athens were citizens. Citizenship was only open to free adult men whose parents were Athenian. Women, slaves, and foreigners were not eligible for citizenship. In 451 B.C.E. the population of Athens was about 300,000. This included about 75,000 slaves, 45,000 foreigners, 100,000 children of citizens, and 35,000 wives of citizens. Only 45,000 residents—about 15 percent of the population—were actually citizens and eligible to vote.

To make sure that no one person could become too powerful, the Athenian democratic system had a safeguard. Once a year a special vote was held in the Assembly. Any citizen present at the meeting could choose the man he most wanted to have leave Athens, and write that man's name on a ballot. If 6,000 or more citizens named one person, that man had to leave Athens for 10 years. No charges had to be made against him, much less proven; he just had to leave.

Adapted from *Hands-on Culture of Ancient Greece and Rome.*

Main idea, paragraph 1: _____

Relevant to topic? Yes _____ No _____

Main idea, paragraph 2: _____

Relevant to topic? Yes _____ No _____

LESSON 12
Preparing Content Cards

Now you're ready to take notes on your reading. An organized approach will make a big difference. When you take notes from different sources, it can be hard to keep track. As you write the report, you may not know which source a quotation came from. The approach described here will help you keep track.

This system uses 3 × 5 cards, with one card for every fact or idea you write down. Yes, this does mean you will have a lot of cards by the time you're done. But this system makes it easy to keep track of which source your notes come from. It also makes it easy to organize your notes when you start preparing an outline.

Content Cards   In Lesson 10, you learned how to set up bibliography cards. Content cards are the other half of the system. Each content card includes four elements: one fact or idea, a code identifying the source it came from, the page number in the source, and a topic header.

1. Start by writing the source code in the upper right-hand corner of the card. This is the source number you assigned to the resource when you made bibliography cards.

2. Below the source code, write the page number where you found the material.

3. In the body of the card, write one fact or idea that you think should go in your paper.

4. Look at your list of main concepts and keywords. These will be the starting point for your topic headings. Does the fact or idea on the card fit under any of these headings? If it does, write that heading at the top of the card. If not, think of a heading that fits the information. Write the heading at the top of the card. Then add it to your list of keywords.

5. As you take notes, be careful to use your own words. If you copy something word for word from the source, put quotation marks around it. Lesson 13 will have more on how to use notes for direct quotations from the source.

Preparing Content Cards *(continued)*

Model   This sample content card is for a project on indentured servants in the American colonies. The material comes from a book on U. S. history, identified as Source #1.

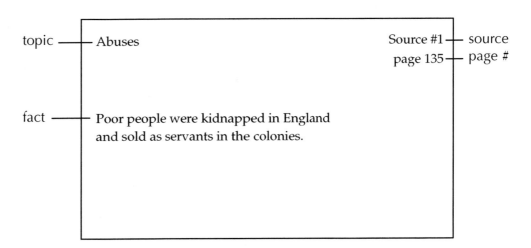

topic —— Abuses   Source #1 —— source
                                                   page 135 —— page #

fact —— Poor people were kidnapped in England
         and sold as servants in the colonies.

Application   This excerpt is from another book on indentured servants. According to the bibliography cards, this book is Source #2. Read the excerpt. Then prepare two content cards for facts or ideas in the text. Remember, you will need to provide topic headings for the cards.

> Most people who came to the early American colonies wanted to be independent. They bought land or set up in business for themselves. This meant that employers found it hard to hire servants or laborers. Most people were working for themselves.
>
> One answer to this problem was found in "indentured servants." These were people who agreed to work in America for a certain number of years. In return, their employer paid for their trip from Europe to the colonies.
>
> Some indentured servants were treated very well. When their time of service was up, their employers gave them tools, seed, and sometimes even land so that they could set up for themselves.
>
> Some servants weren't treated as kindly. Indentured servants could be bought and sold like property. They could not get married without their master's permission. They could not work for someone else. They often had to work very hard and were not fed well.
>
> Some masters branded their indentured servants. Then, if the servants ran away, they were easy to identify. Indentured servants hired out to bad masters often didn't live until the end of their period of service.
>
> *61 Cooperative Learning Activities in U.S. History* by Kate O'Halloran. © 1998 by J. Weston Walch, Publisher.

41 *Content-Area Research Strategies*

Content Card #1:

Content Card #2:

LESSON 13
Plagiarism and Quoting

Plagiarism

In the lesson on taking notes, you learned that you should take notes in your own words. Why shouldn't you copy directly from the source? Because it's easy to end up using someone else's words or ideas in your paper. Even if you only use a sentence or two, you're passing someone else's work off as your own. This is known as *plagiarism.* It is a form of theft: stealing someone else's ideas or words and claiming them as your own.

The best way to avoid plagiarism is to put all your notes in your own words. When you combine the material on the cards into a paper, it will be all your own work.

Quoting

Sometimes, though, you have a really good reason to use the original author's words. Maybe the original wording was so clear, or so clever, that you know your readers will like it. Maybe the author is an expert in the field. That person's words will carry much more weight than yours. You can use the words to back up your argument.

To use someone else's words without plagiarizing, use them as a quotation. First, copy the material from the original source exactly, word for word. Don't even change a comma. The quotation has to be exactly the same as the original.

Now, to make sure you remember that these are someone else's words, put quotation marks at the beginning and end of the quotation. It may even help to highlight the quotation marks. That way you can't mistake a quotation for your own words.

Next, be sure you know exactly whose words they are. Did the author of the book or article say this? Or was that author quoting someone else? Look carefully at the original source to make sure you have the right name. Then write the name on the content card, just below the quotation. This means that you can give credit to the right person if you use the quotation in your paper.

Apart from the quotation marks and the author's name, treat this content card in the usual way. Put the source number in the upper right-hand corner.

Plagiarism and Quoting *(continued)*

Write the page number below that. And write the topic header at the top of the card.

Model   The topic of this paper is "Nixon and Watergate: Bringing out the Truth." The quoted material is from Nixon's address to the nation on April 30, 1973. The student chose to quote this material because it showed a side of Nixon's character. It also reflected the wording of the topic very neatly.

Nixon's Character   Source #6
                                                       page 111

"I was determined that we should get to the bottom
of the matter, and that the truth should be fully
brought out—no matter who was involved."
—Richard M. Nixon

Application   Here is more of the same excerpt. Choose another quotation from this speech for the topic "Nixon and Watergate: Bringing out the Truth." Then prepare a content card for the quotation you chose. Remember to copy the material exactly, including punctuation, to put it in quotation marks, and to include the speaker's name.

You can use the same source code and page number as the card above. However, you may want to give your quotation a different topic head.

Plagiarism and Quoting *(continued)*

Last June 17, while I was in Florida trying to get a few days rest after my visit to Moscow, I first learned from news reports of the Watergate break-in. I was appalled at this senseless, illegal action, and I was shocked to learn that employees of the Re-election Committee were apparently among those guilty. I immediately ordered an investigation by appropriate Government authorities. On September 15, as you will recall, indictments were brought against seven defendants in the case.

As the investigation went forward, I repeatedly asked those conducting the investigation whether there was any reason to believe that members of my Administration were in any way involved. I received repeated assurances that there were not. . . .

Until March of this year, I remained convinced that the denials were true and that the charges of involvement by members of the White House Staff were false. . . . However, new information then came to me which persuaded me that there was a real possibility that some of these charges were true, and suggesting further that there had been an effort to conceal the facts both from the public, from you, and from me.

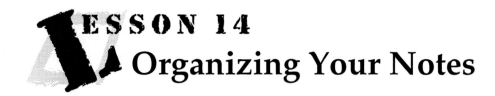

LESSON 14
Organizing Your Notes

Sorting

Finally, all your research is done. You used a variety of sources for your material. You prepared bibliography cards for each source. As you read, you took notes on content cards, coding them to show which source each note came from. Now you have a huge pile of cards in front of you. What on earth are you going to do with them?

Believe it or not, this part is easy. This is where the topic heads you wrote on those cards are useful.

The first step is to separate your bibliography cards from your content cards. Arrange the bibliography cards in numerical order, starting with Source #1. You can set them aside for now; you probably won't need them until you start writing. You may want to put an elastic band around them, to keep them together.

Sort by Topic

Next, check that all your content cards include a topic head. If any cards don't have a head, add one now. Use your main concepts and keywords list to choose an appropriate head.

The next step is like sorting playing cards by suit. You want to group together all the cards that have the same topic head. When you finish, all your cards should be in piles, with one topic per pile.

Sort by Subtopic

Now go through all the cards in each pile, one pile at a time. Read the information on each card. By now you know enough to tell if information on any of the cards is wrong. Get rid of any cards that have wrong information on them.

Do some cards address the same idea as other cards? If so, group them together. Some cards may give details about a fact on another card. Group those cards together.

Arrange the cards in the pile in a way that makes sense. This may be in chronological order—order by time. It may be in order of importance, from most important to least important. It may be some other order. Choose the way that fits best with your information.

Once the cards in one pile are in order, write a number on each card, to the right of the topic head, and circle the number. Number the first card "1," the second card "2," and so forth.

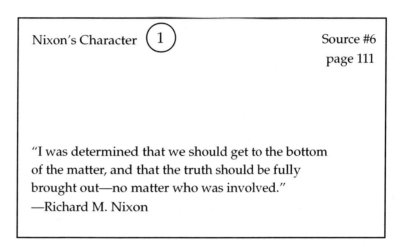

Continue doing this until the cards in all the piles are organized and numbered.

Organizing Your Notes *(continued)*

Application   Here are some of the content cards for a paper on Langston Hughes. The topic head is "Hughes's Childhood." Decide which cards should go together, and what order the cards should be in. Write a number beside each card to show where in the sequence it should go.

___ father thought writing wouldn't pay, wanted more practical career for Langston

___ born February 1, 1902, Joplin, Missouri

___ at 13 moved to Lincoln, Illinois, to live with his mother, her husband

___ soon dropped out of Columbia engineering program, continued to write

___ full name: James Langston Hughes

___ raised by his grandmother until he was 13

___ attended Central High School in Cleveland, Ohio

___ after high school spent a year in Mexico with father

___ began writing poetry in eighth grade, was named class poet

___ father paid tuition at Columbia University to study engineering

___ parents divorced when he was small, father moved to Mexico

___ 1920: finished high school

___ family eventually settled in Cleveland, Ohio

___ spent a year at Columbia University

Content-Area Research Strategies

PART III
Writing the Paper

Choosing a Writing Pattern

Writing Patterns

Any essay can be organized in different ways. However, some ways of organizing writing will work better than others for any given paper. The best way to organize your material depends on several factors:

Audience—who you expect to read the paper

Purpose—the reason you are writing

Topic—the topic you have chosen

Here are some common writing patterns, and situations in which a writer might choose to use them.

Cause and Effect

This type of essay usually explains how or why something happened, and what resulted from it. The "something" can be an event, a problem, a situation, an idea, and so forth. A cause-and-effect pattern can also be used to speculate about possible results if something is done in the future. Use this type of pattern to analyze the relationship between things. Why did it happen? What are its effects? How is it related to something else? Examples: why volcanoes erupt and what happens when they do; why many Europeans immigrated to the United States during the nineteenth century; how the world would look if the ice caps melt and ocean levels rise; why zebra mussels are a problem in the Great Lakes.

Classification

Classification can be used in two ways. One is to explain why a certain thing belongs in a certain class or category. To do this, you show the features that identify things in that class. Then you show that the thing being discussed has those features. The other use of classification involves dividing a group of things into classes. You show that a broad concept can be narrowed down to a more specific one. This pattern is often found in scientific or technical writing. What are a thing's parts or types? How can they be separated or grouped? What categories can they be arranged in? Into what categories can its parts or types be arranged? On what basis can the thing be categorized? Examples: types of governments; renewable and nonrenewable energy sources; planets; plant and animal kingdoms.

Choosing a Writing Pattern *(continued)*

Compare and Contrast

This pattern looks at similarities and differences. It can be used for a discussion of things, events, people, places, ideas, beliefs, and so forth. A compare-and-contrast essay can be used to show the ways things are similar, or the ways they are different. It can show that things that appear unlike each other are actually quite similar. It can show that things that appear similar are actually different. It can be used to argue that one thing is better than another. Use this pattern to evaluate two or more options. How is something like other things? How is it different from other things? Examples: the paintings of Monet and Degas; plants and fungi; climate in coastal and central regions; religions of the world; wise men and fools in Shakespeare's plays.

Persuasive

A persuasive essay tries to persuade the reader to believe something. It may suggest that one point of view is correct. It may argue that one course of action should be taken. It may also be used to convince the reader that something is incorrect or untrue. The persuasive essay presents evidence in support of a point of view. Use this pattern with a topic that has more than one side. Examples: school uniforms in public schools; ethics and the atom bomb.

Sequence

This format presents information in some sort of order. This is often chronological order you present the information in the order it occurred. This type of essay can be used to describe a series of events, a process, or anything else that can be arranged in order. Examples: the life cycle of a salmon; the life and works of Charles Dickens; how to set up a computer database.

Choose a Pattern

Look at your piles of notes. Analyze the topic heads on the cards. Based on these, you should be able to choose an appropriate writing pattern.

Model

Here are one student's topic heads for an essay on World War I.

Conflicting national interests

Problem of military alliances

Growth of military planning

Outbreak of World War I

A cause-and-effect writing pattern would work well for these topic heads. The essay title could be "Long-Range Causes of World War I."

Application

Here are the topic heads for an essay on Langston Hughes. Based on these topics, choose a writing pattern for this essay.

Childhood

Education

Hughes as writer

Hughes as lecturer

Hughes as editor

Hughes and the Harlem Renaissance

Honors & awards

Influences

Legacy

Writing pattern: _____

LESSON 16
Developing the Outline

The outline is the last step before you actually start to write. The outline is a diagram of the essay, from introduction to conclusion. It helps keep you on track as you write the essay.

Standard Outline Structure

The standard format for an outline begins by listing all the main ideas of the essay. These are indicated by a Roman numeral followed by a period: I. Subtopics are listed under each main idea. They are indented (set in) from the main idea, and are indicated by a capital letter followed by a period: A. Under each subtopic, list all the ideas or facts that support the subtopic. These are indented from the subtopic, and are indicated by an Indo-Arabic numeral followed by a period: 1.

I. First main idea

   A. First subtopic for main idea I
      1. First supporting idea for subtopic A
      2. Second supporting idea for subtopic A

   B. Second subtopic for main idea I
      1. First supporting idea for subtopic B
      2. Second supporting idea for subtopic B

II. Second main idea

   A. First subtopic for main idea II
      1. First supporting idea for subtopic A
      2. Second supporting idea for subtopic A

   B. Second subtopic for main idea II
      1. First supporting idea for subtopic B
      2. Second supporting idea for subtopic B

Of course, each main idea can have more than two subtopics, and each subtopic can have more than two supporting ideas. But you should always have at least two subtopics for each main idea, and at least two supporting ideas for each subtopic.

Developing the Outline *(continued)*

Model   Here is an outline for an essay that compares and contrasts two of the world's longest rivers.

I. Nile River

   A. World's longest river
1. Rises near Lake Victoria
2. Flows into Mediterranean Sea
3. Length (mi.): 4,180
4. Length (km): 6,690

   B. Enormous drainage area
1. Sq miles: 1,170,000
2. Sq. km: 2,881,000
3. Includes portions of Tanzania, Burundi, Rwanda, Zaire, Kenya, Uganda, Ethiopia, the Sudan, Egypt
4. Discharge at mouth (cubic meters per second): 1,584

II. Amazon River

   A. World's second-longest river
1. Rises in glacier-fed lakes in Peru
2. Flows into Atlantic Ocean
3. Length (mi.): 3,912
4. Length (km): 6,296

   B. Greatest water flow of any river in world
1. Discharge at mouth (cubic meters per second): 180,000
2. Accounts for about one-fifth of all river water discharged into world's oceans
3. Drainage area (sq. miles): 2,270,000
4. Drainage area (sq. km): 7,180,000

Develop an Outline from Note Cards   This is where your note cards really pay off. The topic heads on your cards will be the main ideas and subtopics for your outline. The information on the cards will be the supporting ideas. You have already organized the cards by topic (main idea or subtopic). Within each topic, you have arranged the cards in sequence. And you have chosen the best writing pattern for your information. Now all you need to do is decide the order of the topic heads, based on

Developing the Outline *(continued)*

the writing pattern. Then write the topic heads and the essential information from each card in outline form.

Application   Here are two topic heads for an essay on Langston Hughes, and some of the facts on the content cards for each topic. Use this information to prepare an outline for the first two paragraphs of an essay.

Childhood

    born February 1, 1902, Joplin, Missouri

    parents divorced when he was small, father moved to Mexico

    raised by his grandmother until he was 13

    at 13 moved to Lincoln, Illinois, to live with mother, her husband

    family eventually settled in Cleveland, Ohio

Education

    attended Central High School in Cleveland, Ohio

    1920: finished high school

    father thought writing wouldn't pay, wanted more practical career for Langston

    father paid tuition at Columbia University to study engineering

    Langston spent a year at Columbia University

    dropped out of Columbia engineering program, continued to write

I. _____

    A. _____

        1. _____

        2. _____

    B. _____

        1. _____

        2. _____

II. _____

    A. _____

        1. _____

        2. _____

    B. _____

        1. _____

        2. _____

LESSON 17
Writing the First Draft

You're now ready to take your note cards and begin writing your paper. No matter which writing pattern you use, your paper should include three parts: an introduction, the body of the paper, and a conclusion.

Introduction

The introduction is the first paragraph of an essay. It states the main idea of the paper. This is also a good place to give some background information about your topic. If your essay uses some terms readers may not be familiar with, you may want to explain them now.

Model

Here is the introduction for an essay on the *Exxon Valdez* disaster.

> The *Exxon Valdez* left the Alyeska Pipeline Terminal at 9:12 P.M. on March 23, 1989. The ship, loaded with 53,094,510 gallons of crude oil, was bound for Long Beach, California. William Murphy stood at the controls. Murphy was an expert pilot, hired to guide the 987-foot ship out of the port. The ship's captain, Joe Hazelwood, was at his side. They had all done this many times before. None of them had any reason to think this time would be any different. But at 12:04 A.M. the *Exxon Valdez* was grounded on a reef, with millions of gallons of oil pouring through its gashed hull into Prince William Sound.

Body

Use the body of your paper to develop your main idea. Each topic pile should become a paragraph in the body of your paper. Use the facts you gathered to support your points with details and examples. Remember, each paragraph should include only one idea.

If your notes include a direct quotation from the source, make sure you show that you are quoting. Put the material in quotation marks. Include a citation so that readers know who actually said it. Lesson 18 gives detailed instructions for using quoted material in your essay.

To connect your paragraphs together, use transition words. These are words that show how the idea in one paragraph is related to the idea in the next one. Here are some examples of transition words.

Writing the First Draft *(continued)*

To show sequence

after   finally   first, second, third   next   then

To compare or contrast

even though   however   nevertheless   on the other hand

To show cause and effect

as a result   consequently   therefore   thus

For additional information

also   furthermore   in addition

Model

Here is part of the body of the *Exxon Valdez* essay.

> Just before midnight, both Captain Hazelwood and Third Mate Gregory Cousins were on the bridge. Captain Hazelwood spoke with Cousins about how to return the ship to its correct course. When the captain left the bridge, at about 11:53 P.M, Third Mate Cousins was the only officer left on the bridge.
>
> However, company policy was clear. At all times, at least two officers should be on the bridge.

Conclusion

The conclusion wraps up the points you have made. It may refer to the idea you stated in the introduction. It may evaluate the information you provided in the body of the essay. It may include a recommendation for the future, or even a prediction.

However, there is one thing a conclusion should never do: It should never introduce new material. The conclusion should tell the reader that you have finished what you had to say.

Model

Here is the conclusion for the *Exxon Valdez* essay.

> The *Exxon Valdez* oil spill was a disaster. The people and animals of Alaska's coast continue to pay the price for the lack of planning that led to the accident. Perhaps, though, this one accident has managed to prevent others. The tighter harbor controls that this disaster prompted may keep many bays and harbors safe in the future.

Writing the First Draft *(continued)*

Checklist

You can use a checklist like this one to make sure your essay is complete.

____ 1. Does my introduction present the main idea of the essay?

____ 2. Do I have a well-developed paragraph for each topic?

____ 3. Does each paragraph contain one idea, and only one?

____ 4. Do I use facts and details to support my statements?

____ 5. Do I use transition words to link my paragraphs?

____ 6. Do I present ideas and information in a logical sequence?

____ 7. Do I present ideas and information clearly?

____ 8. Does my conclusion wrap up the points I made in the essay?

____ 9. Does my essay follow my outline?

____ 10. Have I included all the topics I had identified?

LESSON 18
Handling Quoted Material

Most of the notes you took during your research were in your own words. Still, there were probably some places where you copied the text directly from the source. Sometimes an author expresses something so clearly that you want to use it. Sometimes the author is an expert; using that person's words will make your argument stronger. Sometimes the quotation is from someone well known and the exact words are important.

You copied the material word for word from the source, to make sure you got it right. You put quotation marks around it so that you would remember it was a quotation. You made a careful note of who said it, and where you found it. Now, as you write the body of your paper, you want to include one of these quotations. What do you need to do?

Set off the Quoted Material

The first thing to do is to show that this is someone else's material, not yours. This is easiest to do if you are only quoting a small amount. Then you just put quotation marks at the beginning and end of the quoted material. This shows where your words end and someone else's begin. If there were already quotation marks somewhere in the passage, change them to single quotation marks.

You also need to include a reference—called a *citation*—to the source. One way to do this is to write the author's name in parentheses after the quotation. You also need to include the page number where the quotation can be found in the source. This gives readers enough information to find the details about the source in your bibliography.

Put the citation at the end of the quotation, but before the sentence's final punctuation. Since you included the author's name and the page number on the content card, you have all the information you need for the citation.

> At a press conference in Florida in November 1973, Nixon said that he had not profited from his office. "People have got to know whether or not their president is a crook. Well, I'm not a crook" (Kilpatrick A1). Not everyone was convinced.

You can use this approach when you are quoting just one or two lines of text.

Handling Quoted Material *(continued)*

Summary: Short Quotations

- Quotation marks at beginning and end.
- Change internal quotation marks to single quotation marks.
- Citation at end of quotation, before final punctuation.

Block Quotation

If you are quoting a longer passage, use the block quotation format. Write an introduction to the quotation, ending with a colon. Instead of starting the quotation right after your introductory comment, start it on a new line. Indent the new line one inch from both margins. In a block quotation, you do not need quotation marks at the start and end of the quotation. Of course, you do still need to include a citation. Put it on the last line of the quote, after the final punctuation. The citation format stays the same: the author's name and the page number, in parentheses.

> Carroll Kilpatrick reported on the conference in the *Washington Post:*
>> When asked whether he still thought former aides John D. Ehrlichman and H.R. (Bob) Haldeman were fine public servants, as he once characterized them, Mr. Nixon called them "dedicated, fine public servants, and it is my belief, based on what I know now, that when these proceedings are completed that they will come out all right."
>> But he said it "probably doesn't make any difference whether the grand jury indicts them or not, because unfortunately they have already been convicted in the minds of millions of Americans by what happened before the Senate (Watergate) committee."
>> It was in this context that the President seriously misspoke himself, saying, "I hold that both men and others who have been charged are guilty until we have evidence that they are not guilty." (Kilpatrick A1)

In fact, this passage is a good example of how to use quotations. The author of this piece was a journalist, writing for a newspaper. Rather than repeat everything Nixon said, Kilpatrick summed it up for readers. He only included Nixon's exact words when he thought they were important.

You probably noticed that there were quotation marks in this quotation, showing where Kilpatrick was quoting Nixon's words. Since you don't put quotation marks around the block quotation, there is no need to change quotation marks to single quotation marks.

Handling Quoted Material *(continued)*

Summary: Block Quotes

- No quotation marks needed.
- Indent one inch from both left and right margins.
- Citation at end of quotation, after final punctuation.

Showing Deletions in a Quotation

Sometimes you want to use part of a quotation but you want to leave out some of the original words. Perhaps the first and last sentences are relevant to your essay but the part in the middle isn't. If you quote the whole thing, your reader will have to figure out which is the important part. You can make this easier by trimming the quotation. You just need to show that there is more in the original than you're putting in your paper.

You do this by using ellipses. These are three spaced periods that look like this: . . . They show that something has been left out.

> Nixon's final comment was, "While technically I did not commit a crime . . . I made so many bad judgments."

If you leave out a whole sentence, or the part of a sentence with the period, you have to add a period to the ellipses. Then you end up with: . . . . , four dots, one for the period, three for the ellipses.

> Speaking of former aides John D. Ehrlichman and H.R. Haldeman, Nixon said they were "dedicated, fine public servants. . . . unfortunately they have already been convicted in the minds of millions of Americans by what happened before the Senate (Watergate) committee."

Application

Following is some text giving the background of the Watergate scandal. The author's name is Baker. This excerpt appeared on page 110 of Baker's book. Choose a line or two from the text to quote. Write your own introductory text for the quotation, followed by the quoted material. Don't forget to use quotation marks and include a citation. If you delete any material, show the deletion with ellipses.

Handling Quoted Material *(continued)*

> "Watergate" is the popular name for the political scandal that resulted in President Nixon's resignation in 1974. The scandal began with the arrest of five burglars in the Democratic National Committee headquarters at the Watergate building in Washington, D.C. The diligence and persistence of members of the press and of Judge John Sirica, the judge who tried the burglars, led to disclosures that seemed to connect the burglary and other events to the White House.

Write your introduction and trimmed quotation here.

_____

_____

_____

_____

_____

_____

_____

_____

_____

_____

_____

_____

_____

Use Quotations Sparingly

Quotations can add a lot to your paper. Expert authors can give you extra authority. Quoting historical figures can make history come alive. However, quotations can be overused. If you get carried away, you can end up with a paper that's almost all other people's words. Your words should be the ones a reader is most aware of. Use quotations to add interest, but rely on your own writing to make your points.

LESSON 19
Revising and Editing the Draft

The first draft is written. Whew! You're almost done now. The final stage for the main part of the paper is editing and revising. When you wrote the first draft, you focused on the content. You needed to arrange the material in a way that made sense, with paragraphs, transition words, and quotations. You were concentrating on the parts of the paper.

Now you need to look at the paper as a whole. No matter how careful you are with the first draft, mistakes can slip in. Editing gives you the chance to find those mistakes and fix them.

Revising a draft looks at two kinds of problems. We could call them the big picture and the fine print. When we look at the big picture, we look at the shape and structure of the whole paper. We revise to make sure the essay flows smoothly and makes sense. When we look at the fine print, we check the details: sentences, spelling, word choice. Here are some guidelines for looking at both the big picture and the fine print.

Big-Picture Issues

It's easiest to look at the big picture if you can take a break from the material. Don't finish the draft, then go straight into the revision process. A little time away can help you see things with a fresh eye. Ideally, set the paper aside for a day before starting to revise. If you don't have enough time for that, even half an hour away can help. Go on, take a break; you deserve it.

When you come back, try looking at the big picture—literally. Hold the paper out at arm's length so you can't quite read it. Look at the shapes of the lines on the page. Do you see lots of short, choppy paragraphs? Maybe some of them should be combined into larger ones. Do you see a whole page with barely any paragraph breaks? Your paragraphs may be too long. Make sure each paragraph only has one idea. Do you see lots of big chunks where the text is indented for block quotations? Check that you haven't overused excerpts from other writers.

Revising and Editing the Draft *(continued)*

Now read carefully through the entire paper. Think about it as a whole. Ask yourself questions like these:

- Does the whole paper make sense?
- Does it express my main idea?
- Is the writing pattern appropriate for the topic?
- Do I have an introduction? supporting paragraphs? a conclusion?
- Does each paragraph serve a purpose in the essay as a whole?
- Are the paragraphs in a logical order?
- Do the paragraphs flow smoothly?
- Have I used transition words to link paragraphs?
- Is the paper interesting?

Fine-Print Issues

Once you've made sure the paper works as a whole, it's time to move on to the fine print. Fine-print issues are the small things that can come between you and the reader. If you make spelling and grammar errors, readers may think you could make factual errors, too. If your writing is unclear, readers may not understand your point. Most of these problems can be fixed quite quickly. It's worth putting in the time.

When you looked at the big picture, you used your eyes for an overview. For the fine print, try using your ears. Read the whole paper aloud—s-l-o-w-l-y. Try to listen as you read. You may be surprised by what your ears pick up that your eyes missed before.

Next, try a personalized approach to editing. Most writers have one or two weak spots—even professional writers! There are one or two mistakes that they just keep on making. The "right" version just doesn't seem to come naturally to them. Rather than admit defeat, good writers take note of the areas where they have trouble. Then they look for those issues as they revise their drafts. For example, a writer may use run-on sentences: "A tsunami begins with a tremor of some kind that shakes the bottom of the ocean and causes a wave to form that then travels quickly across the deep ocean until it reaches shallow water near the shore." That writer would go through a piece looking for run-on sentences to rework.

Revising and Editing the Draft *(continued)*

Are there any areas in your writing that you know need attention? Note them down. Work out a way to fix them. Then go through the paper looking for those areas. Some common trouble spots are:

- run-on sentences ("I did this and this and that and then this and . . .")
- sentence fragments ("And then")
- noun/verb disagreement ("We argues . . .")
- inconsistent verb tenses ("It is day. The sky was blue.")
- unnecessary words ("each and every"—could be "each")
- long words ("utilize" instead of "use"; "endeavor" instead of "try")

Once you have checked for your own weak spots, check that all the details are right.

Ask yourself questions like these:

- Have I checked my spelling?
- Are all my sentences clear and complete?
- Have I used punctuation correctly?
- Are all quotations handled appropriately (in quotation marks or set as block quotations)?
- Do I have a complete citation for every quotation?
- Is my choice of words clear and effective?

Use the answers to these questions to revise your first draft.

The Final Draft

Once you've revised your draft, you're almost done. Type or write the final draft. Prepare the Works Cited page, described in Lesson 20. Proofread the whole paper one more time. And that's it! Congratulations on a job well done!

LESSON 20
Preparing the Bibliography

Remember those bibliography cards you prepared? This is where they get put to good use. You've revised the first draft of your paper, and you know exactly which content and quotation cards you used. You need to put that information in writing.

When we looked at evaluating resources, one aspect we considered was documentation. Did the resource document its sources? Was there support for the facts and information in the source? The same test applies to your research paper. You need to be able to back up anything you've said. If readers want to check on something, they should be able to find the information. And the first place they would look would be your bibliography.

A bibliography is a list of the sources you used to get information for your report. It appears on a separate page at the end of the paper. This page can have a variety of titles. For the style we will be using, title the page "Works Cited."

Organizing Entries

When you quoted from these sources in the text, you put a citation in parentheses. This gave the author's last name and the page number in the source. If someone wanted to find the details, they would look for the author's last name. To make it easy to find those details, all sources in the bibliography are listed alphabetically by author. Of course, you only put the author's last name in the citation. The entries here will put the last name first, then the first name.

You will also include details for sources you used but didn't quote. The "Works Cited" page should give information about every resource you used to prepare your paper.

Bibliographic Details

Because of the way they are produced and stored, different types of resources have different bibliographic details. This makes more sense if you remember the point of those details: to help readers find the resources. For example, a specific book was published in May, 2000. It was revised and reissued in October, 2003. But since it was only issued once in 2000 and once in 2003, you don't need to know the month to find the version you want. On the other

Preparing the Bibliography *(continued)*

hand, a daily newspaper is published 365 times a year. If you listed only the year of publication, it would be very hard to find a specific article. You need to know the day of the month that article appeared.

Still, even though the details vary a bit, the basics for every resource are the same. You need to give the author, if an author is named. You need to give the name of the resource. If it was part of a larger work (a newspaper, an encyclopedia) you need to give the name of both the resource and the larger work. You need to say who produced the resource, where it was produced, and when. And you need to give the information in pretty much the order described here.

Preparing Entries

In Lesson 9 you learned how to record bibliographic details for different types of resources. Now we will be organizing those details to fit a standard approach. This includes using quotation marks and underlining for certain elements. Again, there is logic to this. If the resource is a complete work, it is underlined. A book is a complete work, so a book's title is underlined. A magazine is a complete work, so its name is underlined. A movie is a complete work, so . . . you get the message.

But an article in a magazine is not a complete work; it is part of the whole magazine. The same goes for a short story, a poem, an article on a web site, even an episode of a television show. They are all parts of something larger. To make this clear in the bibliography, these smaller parts are written in quotation marks. If you remember that logic, it will be easier to keep the bibliography straight:

- List authors' last names first so that they are easy to find.
- <u>Underline</u> the names of whole works.
- Put the names of partial works "in quotation marks."

Handling the Details

This section describes how to handle some common resource types. First the rule for the structure is given. Parts that should be underlined in the bibliography are underlined in the rule. Parts that should be in quotation marks are shown in quotation marks. In fact, all the punctuation that is in the rule should be in your entry: commas, periods, angle brackets. To show how it works, there is a sample entry after each rule. Copy the style of these entries and your entries will be correct.

Preparing the Bibliography *(continued)*

And just a few more general tips:

- Start each entry at the left margin. Don't put the author on one line, the title on the next, and so forth. Just keep going until you reach the end of the line. Then indent the second line and continue. This makes it easier to see where one entry ends and the next one starts.

- If no author name is given, start with the title of the book, article, and so on.

Books

Book, One Author

Author (last name, first name). <u>Title of the book</u>. City: Publisher, date of publication.

Simpson, Bart. <u>How to Succeed in School</u>. Springfield: Krusty Publishing, 2002.

Book, Two Authors

First author (last name, first name), and Second author (first name, last name). <u>Title of the book</u>. City: Publisher, date of publication.

Burns, Charles, and Maggie Simpson. <u>A Partnership Made in Heaven</u>. Capitol City: Burns Worldwide, 2000.

Book, No Author Named

<u>Title</u>. City: Publisher, date of publication.

<u>The Simpsons Dictionary</u>. Shelbyville: Amadopolis Aristole Press, 2003.

Encyclopedia

Author of Article (if given). "Article Title." <u>Encyclopedia Title</u>, Edition Date.

Flanders, Ned. "Good Neighbors." <u>Encyclopedia D'oh</u>. 2003 ed.

Articles

Magazine

Author (last name first). "Article Title." <u>Name of Magazine</u>. Date: Page(s).

Van Houten, Milhouse. "My Buddy Bart." <u>Clog Dancing Times</u>. 6 Jun, 2001: 17.

Preparing the Bibliography *(continued)*

Newspaper

Author (last name first). "Article Title." <u>Name of newspaper</u>. (date): edition if available, section, page number(s).

Skinner, Seymour. "Hair Care for Today's Man." <u>Springfield Times</u>. 8 Dec. 2000: 1.

Television and Movies

Television program

"Title of Episode or Segment." Credit (Performer or author). <u>Title of Program</u>. Name of Network. Call letters (if any), City of Local Station (if any). Broadcast date.

"Lost Our Lisa." Matt Groening. <u>The Simpsons</u>. FOX. 17 May 1998.

Movie

<u>Title</u>. Director. Distributor, Year.

<u>Who Shot Mr. Burns?</u> Waylon Smithers. Sector 7G Films, 1999.

On-line Resources

Web site

Creator's name (if given), last name first. <u>Web Page Title</u>. Date of latest update. Institution or organization. Date of access. <URL network address>.

Wiggum, Ralph. <u>Eat Paste</u>. 8 Nov. 2002. Springfield Elementary School. 6 Jan. 2003. <http://www.eatpaste.edu/recipes.html>.

Article in On-line Reference

"Article Title." <u>Web Page Title</u>. Date of latest update. Institution or organization. Date of access. <URL network address>.

"The Simpsons as Social Commentary." <u>D'oh Online</u>. Mar. 2002. Encyclopedia D'oh. 29 Mar. 2002 <http://www.doh.com/satire.html>.

Preparing the Bibliography *(continued)*

Article in an On-line Magazine

Author's name (if given). "Title of Article." <u>Name of Magazine</u> Date of Publication. Date of Access <URL network address>.

Borton, Wendell. "Travel Sickness as a Metaphor for Life." <u>Bus Times</u> 1 May 1999. 2 May 1999 <http://www.bigyellowbus.com/fieldtrip.html>.

Model

Here is a sample "Works Cited"page, using some of the resources described above.

Works Cited

Burns, Charles, and Maggie Simpson. <u>A Partnership Made in Heaven</u>. Capitol City: Burns Worldwide, 2000.

Flanders, Ned. "Good Neighbors." <u>Encyclopedia D'oh</u>. 2003 ed.

Simpson, Bart. <u>How to Succeed in School</u>. Springfield: Krusty Publishing, 2002.

Skinner, Seymour. "Hair Care for Today's Man." <u>Springfield Times</u>. 8 Dec. 2000: 1.

Van Houten, Milhouse. "My Buddy Bart." <u>Clog Dancing Times</u>. 6 Jun. 2001: 17.

Wiggum, Ralph. <u>Eat Paste</u>. 8 Nov 2002. Springfield Elementary School. 6 Jan. 2003. <http://www.eatpaste.edu/recipes.html>.

Application

Here are several resources used for a research project. Set them up as a Works Cited page. Remember to organize the list alphabetically, and to put all the details in the right order.

Books

Author: Tony Zurlo
Title: Japan: Superpower of the Pacific
City of Publication: Parsippany, NJ
Publisher: Dillon Press
Date of Publication: 1991

Preparing the Bibliography *(continued)*

Author: Boye DeMente
Title: The Whole Japan Book
City of Publication: Phoenix, AZ
Publisher: Phoenix Book Publishers
Date of Publication: 1983

On-line Resources

Sponsoring Organization: Japan Atlas
URL: http://www.jinjapan.org/atlas/crafts/craft_fr.html
Web Page Title: Japan Crafts
Latest Update: 9/12/02
Date of Access: 11/3/02

PART IV
Excerpts

EXCERPT GROUP A
Glaciers

by J. Grendel

Huge, ancient, and bitterly cold, no one sees it move across the landscape. And yet it slips forward, day by day, creeping down mountain valleys, spreading across the plains. Behind it lies devastation. In places the earth is scraped bare. Elsewhere strange mounds of rock are tumbled in heaps. In more than one place huge semi-circles, like amphitheaters for giants, are scooped from the solid rock of a mountainside.

It sounds like a mythical beast from a science-fiction story, but it's actually very much of our own planet Earth. What is this strange thing? It's a glacier.

Glaciers are huge swaths of compressed ice, often covering hundreds of square kilometers. They form in areas where snow stays on the ground all year. As new snow falls on top of old, the weight of the new snow forms a heavy blanket. The weight slowly squeezes the old snow below, compressing it. Over time many layers of snow build up. The structure of snow in the lower layers begins to change. The crystals form grains, like sugar. The air pockets between the grains become smaller. Although it's not yet ice, this layer is no longer snow.

As more time passes, the lower layers are squeezed into ice. And as more snow falls, and more layers are built, the compressed ice grows thicker. When the ice mass reaches a certain thickness—about 18 meters—the combined effect of weight and gravity forces the ice into motion. The ice is squeezed by its own weight and slowly begins to flow downhill.

Most glaciers move too slowly to be noticed. Some move only a few millimeters a day; some move a few meters. Sometimes a glacier begins to surge forward for weeks, even months. In 1986 the Hubbard Glacier in Alaska began to surge forward, covering about 10 meters a day. Within two months it dammed the mouth of Russell Fiord and created a lake. The fastest glacial surge on record is that of the Kutiah Glacier, in Pakistan. In 1953 it traveled more than 12 km in three months, averaging 112 meters a day.

What happens as the glacier moves forward? Imagine a huge mass of compressed ice, perhaps 20 km long, 2 km wide, and 30 m thick. Even as this mass moves forward, its weight presses it down. Rocks and boulders are scraped up as the ice passes over them. Embedded in the ice, they drag across the land like giant fingernails, leaving deep gouges behind them. Eventually the boulders are flung aside, forming strange landforms, called *moraines*. The eroding action

(continued)

74

Glaciers *(continued)*

Reading 1: The Earth-Shaper (continued)

of the ice can carve valleys through the earth. In some areas, as water levels rise, these valleys fill with water and become fjords. The coast of Norway, with its deep indentations, is eloquent testimony of a glacier's power.

Grendel, J. "The Earth-Shaper." <u>Firn Times</u>, November 4, 2000, p. 35

EXCERPT GROUP A
Glaciers

Reading 2: Glacial Landforms

Glaciers shape the land in two different ways: by erosion and by deposition. These definitions are from the *Dictionary of Glacial Landforms*, published by Bergschrund Press, Oslo, Norway, in 1998.

Erosional Landforms

Arete

When two glaciers erode a mountain ridge from both sides, they form a sharp, narrow ridge.

Cirque

In alpine glaciers, the area where snow first accumulated and developed into a glacier may be eroded to form a shallow depression. As more ice forms, the depression is deepened, until a cirque develops. This is a semicircular depression in the bedrock, shaped like an amphitheater.

Fiord

If a glacier keeps moving, it will eventually meet the sea. At that point, it may form a fiord—a glacial trough whose base is below sea level. The trough fills with seawater, forming a narrow channel.

Hanging Valley

In areas with glacial action, several glaciers may be moving at one time. When a smaller glacier meets a larger one, the two glaciers may become one. But the valley carved by the smaller glacier before they joined will be shallower than that of the larger glacier. When both glaciers retreat they may leave two interconnected valleys with dramatically different depths. The base of the shallower valley may seem to hang above the deeper one.

Horn

Sometimes several glaciers form on the sides of the same mountain, eroding cirques in the rock. As the cirques get bigger, they push deeper into the mountain, eventually creating a pyramid-shaped mountain peak.

Striations

As the glacier moves across bedrock, rocks and other debris embedded in the ice are dragged across the rock, leaving scratches in the rock surface.

U-Shaped Valley

Just as a river of water cuts through the landscape, so does a river of ice. Glaciers often leave deep troughs and valleys in their wake. Where valleys carved by rivers tend to be V-shaped, glacial valleys are U-shaped, with a rounded bottom.

(continued)

Reading 2: Glacial Landforms (continued)

Depositional Landforms

Drumlin

A teardrop-shaped, elongated hill of glacial debris, often found in groups.

Esker

Meltwater within the glacier can form channels in the ice. The meltwater carries sediment, which eventually blocks and fills the tunnel. The retreating ice leaves these "tunnels" of sediment behind as long, linear ridges of sand and gravel.

Kettle Holes

Kettles are curious formations: depressions created by sediment. When large blocks of ice are separated from the main glacier, they may be partially buried in meltwater sediment. The block of ice lasts long enough for the surrounding sediment to solidify. When the ice finally melts, it leaves a hole that often fills with water to become a lake.

Moraine

Accumulations of till that are deposited on the surface, sometimes forming ridges.

Till

Till is the debris carried away by the glacier and deposited elsewhere. Till particles can range from fine silt to large boulders. It is often recognized by large boulders of a different rock type than that found locally; these are called *erratics.*

EXCERPT GROUP A
Glaciers

Reading 3:
Glacier Facts

- About 15,000,000 square kilometers of the earth are covered by glaciers.
- The Greenland ice sheet is about 3 km (1.9 miles) thick and covers 1,726,000 sq km (666,400 sq miles).
- The Antarctic ice sheet is more than 4 km (2.5 miles) thick and covers about 13,000,000 sq km (5,000,000 sq miles).
- Glaciers are even found in places with warm climates, including Africa and Indonesia.
- Glaciers store about 75% of the world's fresh water—more than all the world's lakes, rivers, and groundwater supplies combined.
- If all the ice stored in glaciers melted, the sea would rise by about 70 meters (230 ft).
- Glacier ice crystals can grow to be as large as baseballs.

- Glacial ice looks blue because it is extremely dense; the dense ice absorbs the other colors of the spectrum and reflects only the blue light.
- Antarctic ice shelves may calve icebergs that are over 80 kilometers (50 miles) long.
- The Antarctic ice sheet has been in existence for at least 40 million years.
- It can take hundreds of years to compress snow into glacier ice.
- The ice worm, a relative of the earthworm, has adapted to life in the glacier ice; ice worms die if the temperature goes below 20°F or above 40°F.

"Glacier Facts." <u>Oligochaetes Times</u> 7 Jul 2001. 9 Aug 2002 <http://www. glaciation.org>.

Content-Area Research Strategies

EXCERPT GROUP A
Glaciers

Reading 4:
Glacier Types

Different types of glaciers form in different environments. Here are the most common types.

Ice Sheets—enormous continental masses of glacial ice and snow in Antarctica and Greenland

Ice Shelves—ice sheets that extend over the sea and float on water

Ice Caps—small ice sheets that cover less than 50,000 sq km.

Ice Streams and Outlet Glaciers—channelized glaciers that flow more rapidly than surrounding body of ice

Ice Fields—similar to ice caps, but smaller

Mountain Glaciers—develop in high mountainous regions

Valley Glaciers—originate from mountain glaciers or ice fields; spill down valleys

Piedmont Glaciers—valley glaciers that flow onto a relatively flat area and spread out in bulb-like lobes

Cirque Glaciers—glaciers that occupy semicircular depressions high on sides of mountains

Hanging Glaciers—wide glaciers that cling to steep mountainsides; also called ice aprons

Tidewater Glaciers—valley glaciers that reach out into the sea; as ice breaks off the glacier, generates icebergs

Abingdon, Jane. <u>All About Glaciers</u>. New York: Geological Press, 1998. p. 78.

EXCERPT GROUP B
Famous Mathematicians

Reading 1:
Carl Friedrich
Gauss
(1777–1855)

After the discovery of calculus, the body of mathematical knowledge increased very rapidly. Before Newton's time, the skill of a mathematician could span all mathematical activities, but after the 18th century this became increasingly difficult and by the 19th century, utterly impossible. A mathematician singled out as being the "last complete mathematician," that is, one who could contribute to all the fields of mathematics known in his time, was Carl Friedrich Gauss. Gauss was born in 1777 in Brunswick, Germany, into a poor and uneducated family. By the age of three he was recognized as a prodigy in mathematics, a "wonder child" who could easily correct the mathematical mistakes of his elders. As a schoolboy at age ten he was given the busywork task of computing the sum of the first hundred natural numbers and amazed his schoolmasters by obtaining the correct answer within a few minutes. He had recognized a pattern in the numbers and used it to deduce the fact that the sum of the first n natural numbers is given by the expression $n(n+1)/2$.

The genius of young Gauss was recognized by the local duke of Brunswick, who became his patron for life, sending him to the university and later supporting his research activities.

Despite his obvious talent in mathematics, Gauss entered the University of Göttingen intending to study philology, the science of languages. But on March 30, 1796, he made a discovery that so impressed him with the beauty and power of mathematics that he decided to make it his life's career. Since ancient times the constructibility of regular polygons had been an open question: "Which regular polygons can be constructed using only a straight-edge and compass?" Gauss proved that if $p = 2^{2^n} + 1$ is a prime number for a natural number n, then the p-gon is constructible. In 1801 he published his book on number theory, *Arithmetical Investigations*.

For Gauss, "mathematics was the queen of the sciences, and the theory of numbers was the queen of mathematics."

Another of his early accomplishments was the invention of the method of least squares for finding the best value for a sequence of measurements of the same quantity. He went on to do pioneering work in theoretical astronomy, the study of electromagnetism, complex number theory, probability, and the study of special geometrical surfaces. His work on surfaces resulted in the branch of mathematics we now call differential geometry. Gauss had both a geometry named after him as

(continued)

Famous Mathematicians *(continued)*

> ### *Reading 1: Carl Friedrich Gauss* **(continued)**

well as a probability distribution. In 1807 he assumed the position of director of the observatory at Göttingen and kept this position until his death in 1855.

Gauss was clearly recognized as the greatest mathematician of the nineteenth century. He has since been ranked along with Newton and Archimedes as one of the three greatest mathematicians of all time. Perhaps the most appropriate honorary title bestowed upon him was the one given by the king of Hanover; he called Gauss the Prince of Mathematics, a position he has retained over the years.

Frank J. Swetz. *Learning Activities from the History of Mathematics.* Portland, ME: J. Weston Walch, Publisher. 1994. pp. 56–57.

EXCERPT GROUP B
Famous Mathematicians

**Reading 2:
Sonya
Kovalevskaya
(1850–1891)**

In the middle of the nineteenth century, Russia was in a great state of social and economic turmoil. The serfs had been freed, education was modernized, and emphasis on industrialization increased. Into this time of change was born a woman, Sonya Krukovsky Kovalevskaya, who herself would become an agent of change. Her family were aristocrats, landholders with large estates. Her father was a retired general of artillery. As was appropriate for a girl of her social status, she received her early education at home attended by governesses and tutors.

Peter, a favorite uncle who visited frequently, enjoyed talking about mathematics; from listening to him, Sonya developed a special reverence for this "mysterious science." A curious incident in childhood also helped to introduce her to mathematics. The family's country house was renovated and its rooms wallpapered. When Sonya's room was being done, the contractor ran out of wallpaper, so some old lecture notes from General Krukovsky's student days were pasted on the wall. These were calculus notes, and Sonya spent many hours reading and trying to decipher the strange symbols and formulas on her wall. When in 1865 she finally received formal instructions in calculus, she amazed her teachers

by her comprehension of the subject.

Although university reforms of 1860 permitted women to attend lectures, by 1862 these reforms had been repealed and women could no longer attain a higher education in Russia. If Russian women wished to pursue further studies they had to go abroad. To make this situation even more difficult, unmarried Russian women were not permitted to travel outside of Russia. An intellectual marriage of convenience was arranged. Sonya married another young student, Vladimir Kovalevsky, a talented writer. In 1869 they traveled to Heidelberg, Germany, where Sonya Kovalevskaya finally could study mathematics.

She did well in her studies, but after a year she went on to Berlin to study under the great mathematician Karl Weierstrass (1815–1897). At the University of Berlin women were still not allowed to attend lectures, so Weierstrass had to instruct Kovalevskaya privately. At first he was skeptical of a woman mathematician, so he gave her a set of difficult problems to solve, hoping the task would drive her away from mathematics. However, she easily found solutions for the problems and demonstrated her great talent to Weierstrass, who for the next several years became her teacher.

(continued)

Famous Mathematicians *(continued)*

Reading 2: Sonya Kovalevskaya **(continued)**

By 1874 Kovalevskaya had adequately demonstrated an ability to do original mathematics and obtained a doctorate from the University of Göttingen. For a brief period she returned to St. Petersburg and enjoyed married life with her husband. They had a daughter and Kovalevsky became a professor of paleontology at the University of Moscow. Unrest then swept Russia. Kovalevsky became involved in a failing business and committed suicide. At about this time the University of Stockholm was founded. The head of its faculty of mathematics was a former student of Weierstrass and knew of Sonya Kovalevskaya's mathematical talent; he invited her to join the new faculty. She arrived in Stockholm in 1883 and became the first woman university lecturer in Sweden.

In 1888 Kovalevskaya's research paper "On the Rotations of a Solid Body About a Fixed Point" won the grand prize for scientific accomplishment offered by the French Academy of Science. Besides obtaining this great honor and winning a handsome purse of 5,000 francs, Kovalevskaya became the toast of Paris, the intellectual capital of Europe. She was openly acknowledged as a great woman mathematician. Her struggles and sacrifices had borne fruit, and her reputation would now open opportunities for other women to study mathematics.

Throughout her life, Kovalevskaya was also closely associated with literature. She enjoyed writing and likened the creative spirit of poetry to that of mathematics. In 1891, at only 40 years old, Sonya Kovalevskaya died of pneumonia.

Frank J. Swetz. *Learning Activities from the History of Mathematics.* Portland, ME: J. Weston Walch, Publisher. 1994. pp. 68–69

EXCERPT GROUP B
Famous Mathematicians

Reading 3: Srinivasa Ramanujan (1887–1920)

In 1976, an American mathematician, George Andrews, was searching through some old papers stored in a library at Cambridge University. He came across a worn notebook of hand-written pages. The notebook belonged to the Indian mathematician Srinivasa Ramanujan and contained work he accomplished during the last year of his life when he was dying of tuberculosis in Madras. Its contents were extraordinary and have been described as "the equivalent of a lifetime of work of a very great mathematician." Material from this "Lost Notebook" has aided in the development of a new branch of theoretical physics, super-string theory, and one of its mathematical identities was used to devise a computer program that estimated π to an accuracy of several million digits. Who was this Indian mathematician whose work had such an impact long after his death?

Ramanujan was born into a middle-class Indian family in 1887. His father was an accountant for a cloth merchant, and his mother was recognized for her ability in astrology. He was brought up within the strict Hindu prescriptions of the Brahman caste. As a child he was described as being quiet, thoughtful, and possessing an exceptional memory. He would entertain his friends by reciting lists of Sanskrit roots as well as mathematical values for π and the square root of 2 to many decimal places. When he was 15 years old, a friend lent him a copy of Carr's *A Synopsis of Pure Mathematics*. This was mainly a book of algebraic and trigonometric formulas, but it was the first book of higher mathematics that Ramanujan had ever seen.

He set about proving the formulas and enjoyed this new activity. Thus his love for mathematics was born. Frequently he would credit his mathematical discoveries to the family goddess Namagiri, who Ramanujan said appeared to him in dreams. At age 16 he began college, aided by a government scholarship; however, within a year he lost this scholarship by failing an English test. He spent all his efforts on doing and studying mathematics. With the loss of the scholarship his formal education temporarily ended. Despite the lack of academic or scientific support, he continued his mathematical explorations, computing on a slate and recording his final results in notebooks. In 1909 he was married and accepted a position as a clerk in the Madras Port Trust. By 1911 he began publishing mathematical findings in local journals and attracted attention for his unusual results.

(continued)

Content-Area Research Strategies

Famous Mathematicians *(continued)*

Reading 3: Srinivasa Ramanujan (continued)

Several friends suggested he write to G. H. Hardy (1877–1947) at Trinity College, Cambridge, then one of the most famous mathematicians in the English-speaking world. In 1913 Ramanujan sent Hardy some of his mathematic results and sought advice on the work. Hardy was overwhelmed by what he read in this correspondence from an unknown Indian office clerk. Some of the results had been already proven by great mathematicians; others were unknown, and Hardy had to work hard to arrive at their mathematical truth. Hardy obtained financial assistance for Ramanujan to come to Cambridge to study with him. During the next five years the Indian genius studied with Hardy at Cambridge and pursued his mathematical researches; but in 1917 he became ill and was diagnosed as having tuberculosis, an incurable disease at that time.

Despite his illness, Ramanujan's mind remained sharp and his interest in mathematics keen. Once while visiting Ramanujan's sickbed, Hardy said that he had arrived in a taxi that bore the dull number 1729. The bedridden patient responded that no, the number was really interesting, as it could be represented as the sum of two cubes in two different ways: $9^3 + 10^3 = 1{,}729 = 12^3 + 1^3$. Much of Ramanujan's work concerned number theory. J. E. Littlewood, a colleague of Hardy, noted of the Indian mathematician that "each of the positive integers was one of his personal friends." In 1919 Ramanujan returned home to India to die. During this final year of life, he produced his last notebook.

Frank J. Swetz. *Learning Activities from the History of Mathematics.* Portland, ME: J. Weston Walch, Publisher. 1994. pp. 71–72.

EXCERPT GROUP B
Famous Mathematicians

**Reading 4:
Sophie
Germain
(1776–1831)**

In 1801 when *Arithmetical Investigations,* the great work of Carl Friedrich Gauss (1777–1855) on number theory, first appeared, it attracted correspondence for its author. Other members of the mathematical community working in number theory now sought the advice and assistance of Gauss. One such letter, which contained some very interesting findings, was signed simply M. Le Blanc, Polytechnique student. Gauss was deeply impressed with the quality of the work and amazed that an unknown student from the French École Polytechnique could produce work of such standards. He began a correspondence with the Mysterious Monsieur Le Blanc (Mr. White) that lasted several years.

Another contemporary mathematician, Joseph Louis Lagrange (1736–1813), also had encountered Monsieur Le Blanc, but on a more personal, revealing basis. Lagrange at this time was the instructor of mathematical analysis at the École Polytechnique in Paris, the famous French institution for the training of mathematicians and scientists. As was the custom, at the end of each term students at the Polytechnique submitted reports to their professors commenting on the studies completed and presenting their own findings and conclusions on the subjects in question. Lagrange received one such report from

M. Le Blanc and was so impressed by the mathematics accomplished that he personally sought out the author to congratulate him on the excellent caliber of his work. Imagine the great Lagrange's surprise when he discovered that Monsieur Le Blanc was really a woman, Sophie Germain, who due to the prohibition of women studying at the Polytechnique, was forced to assume a male pseudonym. Germain could not even attend Lagrange's lectures; she absorbed his teaching through self-study from a set of notes. This situation was typical of the period. Women could not formally study higher mathematics no matter how bright or talented they were. In fact, Germain had taught herself Latin, Greek, and mathematics from books in the library of her father, a well-to-do merchant. Now she feared that if she wrote to Lagrange under her own name, he would ignore the correspondence, realizing she was a woman; thus, she resorted to deception. She later used this same ruse on Gauss. Lagrange was taken with her apparent talent and interest in mathematics. He praised her as a promising young mathematician of the future and openly introduced her to other leading French scientists. Germain began a broader scientific correspondence among these new acquaintances.

(continued)

Reading 4: Sophie Germain (continued)

In a similar manner, still fearful of her feminine status in the world of mathematics, she began a correspondence with Gauss as M. Le Blanc. It was not until the dramatic events of 1806 that Gauss would learn the true identity of his talented correspondent. In that year, Napoleon's troops occupied the German state of Brunswick and attacked the city of Hanover, home of Gauss. Germain, worried about Gauss's well-being, requested the commanding French officer, a personal friend, to provide for the mathematician's safety, which he did. Gauss was puzzled as to the identity of his benefactress, one Mademoiselle Sophie Germain. What was her interest in him? The mystery was solved in later correspondence with M. Le Blanc when Germain finally admitted her true identity.

Germain continued her work in number theory and also achieved recognition for accomplishments in the field of applied mathematics, where she investigated problems on the transmission of sound and the theory of vibrations. In particular she won a top prize from the French Academy of Science in 1816 for her mathematical theories explaining Chladni figures, which are displayed when a layer of sand is placed on vibrating plates. The phenomenon was first observed and studied by the German physicist Ernst Chladni (1756–1827).

Gauss and Germain never met personally. In 1831 Gauss arranged for Germain to receive an honorary doctorate in science from the University of Göttingen in recognition of her work in mathematics. For a woman this was an unheard-of honor. Unfortunately Germain died of cancer before receiving the degree.

Frank J. Swetz. *Learning Activities from the History of Mathematics.* Portland, ME: J. Weston Walch, Publisher. 1994. pp. 53–54.

EXCERPT GROUP C
Ancient Civilizations

Reading 1:
Mesopotamia

One of the world's first civilizations developed in the area between the Tigris and Euphrates rivers. We call this region Mesopotamia, which means "between the rivers." Early people discovered that they could grow crops on the fertile soil near the rivers. Settlements began to develop.

By about 5000 B.C.E. an early civilization, known as Sumer, had developed here. The Sumerians had learned how to use irrigation to grow more crops. They dug channels to carry the river water to their fields. They grew a variety of crops and raised domestic animals for meat, milk, butter, and leather. They built towns, then cities such as Uruk and Ur, enclosed by walls and featuring ziggurats—huge stepped pyramids with flat tops. Temples were built on top of the ziggurats.

The Sumerians made many technological developments. The development of the plow made cultivating soil easier; the potter's wheel improved utensils for eating and cooking. The ox yoke made it possible to use oxen for hauling. Soon the Sumerians were trading their surplus food and goods with other peoples in the region.

Historians believe that trade and commerce led to the next major developments in Mesopotamia. Traders needed to keep track of their goods; they needed a system of numbers, and a way of writing. The Sumerian numerical system was based on multiples of 60. Traces of this system are still part of our culture today: we count time—seconds and minutes—in units of 60. Their writing system used reed pens to make marks on clay tablets. The reeds made wedge-shaped marks, so historians call this script *cuneiform*, which means wedge-shaped.

Around 2000 B.C.E. a new force arose in Mesopotamia. The city of Babylon grew powerful. In about 1790 B.C.E. Hammurabi became king of Babylon. He conquered other lands in the area, including Sumer, and formed a Mesopotamian empire. To govern the empire he had all the laws of the land written down on stone pillars and clay tablets; known as the Code of Hammurabi, this is the oldest known legal code.

This was a golden age in Babylon. The Babylonians used highly developed geometry, and created epic poetry. The world's first known map dates from this time. But under the rule of Hammurabi's son Babylon declined. By 1590 B.C.E. Babylon had been sacked, and the Mesopotamian empire had come to an end.

From *The Land of Gilgamesh*, by H. Enlil. Published by Fertile Crescent Books, New York, New York, 1992. pp. 17–18

EXCERPT GROUP C
Ancient Civilizations

Reading 2:
Egypt

The land of Egypt is dry. For six months of the year, there is no rain. Over the course of the other six months, a total of one inch falls. Most of the land is desert. And yet a swath of fertile land runs down the center of the country. This is the Nile River, the source of civilization in Egypt.

The Nile flows about 4,100 miles from its source in the mountains to the Mediterranean Sea. Each year heavy rains fall in the mountains, swelling the river. As it sweeps down through Egypt, it overflows. The silt that the river spread over the flooded land created a band of fertile soil.

Unlike other rivers, the Nile floods on a predictable schedule. The waters begin to rise early in July and continue rising until they overflow the river's banks; the flood reaches its crest in September. By the end of October the river is once again within its banks.

By around 5000 B.C.E., towns began to form along the Nile. By 4000 B.C.E. the people had begun to dig irrigation channels to bring the water from the river to the fields. Now, even though no rain fell, they could water their crops. They also harnessed the river for transportation; by 4000 B.C.E. the first sails appeared on boats on the Nile. By 3200 B.C.E. a writing system had developed in Egypt, called hieroglyphics.

Soon two Egyptian kingdoms emerged. The kingdom of Lower Egypt encompassed the lands near the Nile Delta, where the river flows into the Mediterranean. The kingdom of Upper Egypt ran southward along the Nile as far as the first cataract, where the river became unnavigable. Around 3100 B.C.E., the pharaoh, or ruler, of Upper Egypt united the two kingdoms. He founded the First Dynasty of Egypt, and built a capital at Memphis.

Under the pharaohs Egypt grew into a centralized, bureaucratic state. All power was centered in the pharaoh. He owned all the land, controlled the irrigation system, and received the surplus from the crops produced on the royal estates. He taxed the people of Egypt, then used this money to support the court and the kingdom's religious and administrative systems: the administrators, priests, scribes, artists, artisans, and merchants.

The scribes were particularly important in this system. They kept track of the crops the pharaoh received, and the taxes that were paid. They kept records of the dates of the Nile floods in order to predict the flooding more accurately. The development of papyrus—a kind of paper made of reeds—and ink made this record-keeping easier.

(continued)

Reading 2: Egypt (continued)

Around 2650 B.C.E. the age of pyramids in Egypt began. Pyramids were huge stone tombs built for the pharaohs. Scientists and historians are still uncertain how these immense monuments were built with the technology the Egyptians had available.

Of course, the Egyptians had developed a body of scientific knowledge. They had begun to make systematic astronomical observations, and had introduced a 365-day calendar. To measure land and to track the Nile floods they used complex mathematical processes. They used simple machines—such as the shaduf, a lever-based irrigation tool—to perform difficult tasks.

They also developed an understanding of medicine. The first doctor in the world that we know by name—Imhotep—lived around 2650 B.C.E. One of the world's earliest medical textbooks was written by Egyptian surgeons. It explains how to treat broken bones, tumors, and wounds.

They had also developed a body of literature, and libraries to keep their books in. The first book in the form of a novel, "The Story of Sinuhe," dates from about 1900 B.C.E. The "Book of the Dead" collected religious practices and documents.

"The People of the River," by H. A. Shepsut, in *Egyptian Chronicles* magazine, Spring 2002 issue, page 47.

EXCERPT GROUP C
Ancient Civilizations

**Reading 3:
The Indus
Civilization**

The Indus River flows down from the steep mountains of the Hindu Kush, crossing a dry, flat, almost treeless plain on its way to the Arabian Sea. Along the fertile banks of the river, a civilization developed around 2500 B.C.E. The people dug canals to control the river's floods; soon, settlements along the river developed into cities. Two of the largest cities were called Harappa and Mohenjo-Daro. Mohenjo-Daro was about one square mile in size; some 5,000 people lived there.

These cities were built according to an organized plan. The streets were laid out in a grid pattern, which divided the city into rectangular blocks. The buildings were made of baked brick, with flat roofs. The baked bricks were more durable than the sun-dried bricks used in other early civilizations.

At the center of Mohenjo-Daro was a fortress, or citadel. The city also had a large, centrally heated public bath area. Other main buildings included a granary, assembly halls, and towers. Most houses had bathrooms and toilets, with pipes leading to drains that ran under the street. Remains have been found of potter's kilns, dyer's vats, and metalworking, bead making, and shell-working shops.

The people of the Indus Civilization traded with a wide area. Indus Valley clay seals have been found in Sumer. However, historians have not yet been able to decipher the writing system they used, so many details about the civilization remain unknown. We do know that the civilization thrived for about 1,000 years. Around 1700 B.C.E. the Indus River changed its course, which led to severe flooding. Evidence of severe earthquakes has also been found. These events led to the end of the Indus Valley civilization.

"The Lost Civilization." *Encyclopedia Hibernica,* 1997 edition.

EXCERPT GROUP C
Ancient Civilizations

**Reading 4:
Huang He
(Yellow
River)**

The Huang He, or Yellow River, the second-longest river in China, rises in western China and empties into the Bohai Sea. As it passes through China the river collects sediment—over a billion tons of sediment a year. The water becomes literally "yellow."

When the river floods, this sediment is deposited on the land, making it a fertile area for growing crops. The flooding also provides a form of natural irrigation, which helps farming.

This combination of fertile soil and natural irrigation made the Yellow River valley a good place for early farmers. Archeologists have found traces of civilizations here that date back to 5000 B.C.E. Rice cultivation in the area dates to about the same time. By 3000 B.C.E. farmers here had developed the plow, making cultivation easier.

According to legend, the first civilization here was the Xia dynasty. The first Xia emperor, Yu, tamed the Yellow River by building banks to keep the flood at bay and clearing the river channel to facilitate drainage.

However, we have no written records from this time to show that the Xia kingdom actually existed. Also, current evidence makes it unlikely that Yu could really have tamed the river. The sediment in the river is so great

that, even today, dredging cannot keep the channel clear. The Yellow River continues to flood, earning it the nickname "China's Sorrow."

The first dynasty we know of for certain was the Shang kingdom, which arose around 1700 B.C.E. Although it was centered on the Yellow River valley, this civilization's influence extended over a wide area. The Shang developed advanced techniques for casting metal, which they used to create sacred vessels, weapons, and fittings for chariots. They also learned how to make silk textiles, cultivating silkworms and spinning the thread to create elegant cloth. According to tradition, this technique was discovered by the Empress Hsi-Ling Shi, wife of the legendary "Yellow Emperor," Huang Ti. At any event, silk was considered so valuable that the Chinese kept the technique secret for about 3,000 years.

The emperors of the Shang were both political leaders and religious leaders. They had the power to call on their ancestors for advice and information about the future. To do this, a Shang priest would scratch a question into a bone or tortoise shell. The bone was heated, then pressed with hot metal tools. This caused the bone to

(continued)

Reading 4: Huang He (Yellow River) **(continued)**

crack. The priest would then interpret the pattern created by the cracks to answer the emperor's question. This answer was then inscribed on the bone. Their writing system was probably developed around 2800 B.C.E., but the earliest surviving records date to about 1500 B.C.E.

In the later Shang period, the kings grew weak. Around 1000 B.C.E. the Zhou conquered the Shang. The new dynasty ruled China for the next 800 years.

"The Xia and the Shang." *On-Line History of China.* http://www.china.cn. Last updated January 2003. Site accessed March 3, 2003.

EXCERPT GROUP D
S. E. Hinton

Reading 1:
About
S. E. Hinton

Susan Eloise Hinton's career as an author began while she was still a student at Will Rogers High School in Tulsa, Oklahoma. Disturbed by the divisions among her schoolmates into two groups—the Greasers and the Socs—Hinton wrote *The Outsiders*, an honest novel told from the point of view of a Greaser named Ponyboy Curtis. Since her narrator was male, Hinton used only her first initials in case male readers might be put off by a young woman writing from a boy's perspective.

Because of its powerful portrayal of the thoughts and feelings of teenagers, *The Outsiders* became the best-selling young adult novel of all time. Today there are more than eight million copies in print, and the book was made into a feature film.

S. E. Hinton continued to write, producing such smash successes as *That Was Then, This Is Now; Rumble Fish; Tex;* and *The Puppy Sister.* She still lives in Tulsa, with her husband and teenage son. She enjoys riding horses, writing, and taking courses at the university.

In a wonderful tribute to Hinton's distinguished thirty-year writing career, the American Library Association and *School Library Journal* bestowed upon her their first annual Margaret A. Edwards Award, which honors authors whose "book or books, over a period of time, have been accepted by young people as an authentic voice that continues to illuminate their experiences and emotions, giving insight into their lives."

Monica Wood. *Best Books by S. E. Hinton.* Portland, ME: J. Weston Walch, Publisher. 1999. p. ix.

EXCERPT GROUP D
S. E. Hinton

You were a sixteen-year-old high school student in Oklahoma when you wrote *The Outsiders*. How did you pursue getting it published?

I was actually fifteen when I first began it. It was the year I was sixteen and a junior in high school that I did the majority of the work. When I wrote it I had no idea of getting it published. At school one day I mentioned to a friend that I wrote, and she mentioned to me that her mother wrote children's books. She said, "Why don't you let my mother read your stuff?" I gave her a copy of *The Outsiders,* and this woman showed it to a friend of hers who had a New York agent. She said, "Send this to my agent. Maybe she can get it published for you." I didn't believe that was going to happen, but I mailed it to her. She has been my agent ever since.

***The Outsiders* made some pretty strong statements about the importance of school, of books, and of experiencing the world outside of your neighborhood and your clique. Were you consciously trying to send those messages to your readers?**

No. I look back and I think it was totally written in my subconscious or something. I was mad about the social situation in my high school, and I've always been an introspective person. A lot of Ponyboy's thoughts were my thoughts. He's probably the closest I've come to putting myself into a character. I didn't have any grand design. I just sat down and started writing it.

When you wrote *The Outsiders*, did you have any sense that it would become a success?

No, because I wasn't thinking about it for publication; I was writing it for myself. That's the best way to write a book.

You have a son who is right around Ponyboy's age. What does he think of the book, and of having a famous author for a mom?

His class read it in school last year. I'd asked him not to read it before then. It's not the kind of thing he'd pick up to read, anyway. He's into science fiction and fantasy. He said, "Everybody seemed to like it. I didn't hear anybody say they didn't." But he's grown up with it. In grade school he came home one day and said, "You know, Mom, having S. E. Hinton for a mother is like having [President] George Bush for a father." And I said, "I assure you, honey, George Bush is not your father."

(continued)

Reading 2: Talking with S. E. Hinton (continued)

You must get thousands of letters from young people about your books. What do kids say about *The Outsiders*?

Most kids say, "I didn't know anybody else felt that way. I didn't think I was going to like this book, but I just loved it." They're not going to sit around and tell each other they watch sunsets. That's totally uncool. And reading a book is such a private experience. It's a mind connection. I really feel that the emotional intensity is what they respond to.

Have their reactions changed over time?

No. The concept of the "in" group and the "out" group remains the same. The uniforms change, and the names of the groups change, but they really grasp that right away. They say, "OK, this is like the Preppies and the Punks," or whatever they call them.

What books and authors inspired you to become a writer?

Well, as an adult, I can pick out a lot of authors who have influenced me. But people want to know your childhood influences, and I'll have to say just books in general. I loved to read, and as soon as I learned how I was reading everything I could get my hands on. I was a horse nut, and *Peanuts the Pony* was the first book I ever checked out of the library. I still remember that book. The act of reading was so pleasurable and such a connection. For an introverted kid, it's

a means of communication, because you interact with the author even if you aren't sitting there conversing with [him or her]. Books and reading were the largest influences on my writing, but I can't name any book or author that changed my life.

If you were to revisit the characters from *The Outsiders* as adults, where do you think they'd be today?

I always say I'll never write a sequel, so I have no grand scenario planned out. Soda was killed two weeks before his nineteenth birthday in Vietnam. His friend Steve came back from Vietnam a heroin addict and he's been married twice and divorced twice. But now he's a drug counselor. Darry owns a successful construction business. Ponyboy is an expatriate writer. He writes mysteries under the name P. M. Curtis.

When this book came out it shocked a lot of people. Did that surprise you?

No. Because every teenager feels that adults have no idea what's going on. That's exactly the way I felt. I was pleased that they were shocked. One of my reasons for writing it was that I wanted something realistic written about teenagers. At that time there was no realistic teenage fiction. If you didn't want to read "Mary Jane Goes to the Prom" and you were through with horse books, there was nothing to read. I just wanted to write something that dealt with what I saw kids really doing.

(continued)

S. E. Hinton *(continued)*

Reading 2: Talking with S. E. Hinton (continued)

You were a pioneer in writing realistic teen fiction, and as a result didn't get a lot of notoriety or appreciation when you wrote *The Outsiders*. Does that bother you?

No. I'm glad that did not happen. It's very, very satisfying to have a success that's been based on word of mouth. *The Outsiders* was not any overnight, quick-to-the-top-of-the-list sensation. It built gradually, from teachers telling teachers and kids telling kids, and it is a really great satisfaction that *The Outsiders* is where it is today.

Monica Wood. *Best Books by S. E. Hinton.* Portland, ME: J. Weston Walch, Publisher. 1999. pp. ix–x.

EXCERPT GROUP D
S. E. Hinton

**Reading 3:
Books by
S. E. Hinton**

The Outsiders

Ponyboy is caught up in gang rivalry, with tragic consequences. First published: 1967

That Was Then, This Is Now

16-year-old Mark and Byron have always been as close as brothers. Now their different attitudes to life are pulling them apart. First published: 1971

Rumble Fish

Tough guy Rusty-James, a boy who uses his fists more than his brains, relies on his big brother Motorcycle Boy to bail him out when he gets into something he can't handle. But when everything falls apart in an explosive chain of events, Motorcycle Boy isn't there. First published: 1975

Tex

Fifteen-year-old Tex is easygoing and thoughtless. He enjoys his life— if only his brother Mason would stop complaining about the long absence of their father, who has been gone for five months. But Tex seems to attract trouble, and suddenly his world is falling apart. First published: 1979

Taming the Star Runner

When Travis is sent to stay with his uncle in the country, his cool city attitude alienates schoolmates. He finds friendship of a sort with Casey, who runs a riding school and tries to tame the wild and dangerous horse Star Runner. First published: 1979

The Puppy Sister

Aleasha the puppy loves her new family, but she wants to play human games with Nick. Even though Miss Kitty tells Aleasha she can never be a person, Aleasha won't give up without trying. First published: 1995

Big David, Little David

When Nick meets a kindergarten classmate with the same name as his father, and a similar appearance, he wonders if they could be the same person. First published: 1995

"The Books of S. E. Hinton," by Michael Goode. *Reading and Writing,* Summer 1998 issue, pages 17 and 18.

EXCERPT GROUP D
S. E. Hinton

Reading 4: Awards for S. E. Hinton's Books

The Outsiders
New York Herald Tribune Best Teenage Books List, 1967
Chicago Tribune Book World Spring Book Festival Honor Book, 1967
Media and Methods Maxi Award, 1975
ALA Best Young Adult Books, 1975
Massachusetts Children's Book Award, 1979

That Was Then, This Is Now
ALA Best Books for Young Adults, 1971
Chicago Tribune Book World Spring Book Festival Honor Book, 1971
Massachusetts Children's Book Award, 1978

Rumble Fish
ALA Best Books for Young Adults, 1975
School Library Journal Best Books of the Year, 1975
Land of the Enchantment Award, New Mexico Library Association, 1982

Tex
ALA Best Books for Young Adults, 1979
School Library Journal Best Books of the Year, 1979
New York Public Library Books for the Teen-Age, 1980

American Book Award Nomination, 1981
Sue Hefly Honor Book, Louisiana Association of School Librarians, 1982
California Young Reader Medal Nomination, 1982
Sue Hefly Award, Louisiana Association of School Librarians, 1983

Taming the Star Runner
ALA Best Books for Young Adults, 1979
School Library Journal Best Books of the Year, 1979
New York Public Library Books for the Teen-Age, 1980
American Book Award Nomination, 1981
Sue Hefly Honor Book, Louisiana Association of School Librarians, 1982
California Young Reader Medal Nomination, 1982
Sue Hefly Award, Louisiana Association of School Librarians, 1983

The Puppy Sister
Parent's Choice Silver Honor Book, 1995

Online Guide to Best Books. Last revised January 1, 2000. Accessed November 15, 2002. http://www.bestbooks.edu

PART V

Graphic
Organizers

Research Project Schedule

Assignment date: _____

Due date: _____

Step-by-step research and writing	% of time	date you will finish
Step 1: Planning the process	5%	
Step 2: Choosing a topic	10%	
Step 3: Finding the focus for your topic	20%	
Step 4: Gathering information	25%	
Step 5: Preparing to write	10%	
Step 6: Writing and revising	30%	

Content-Area Research Strategies

Blank Brainstorming Web

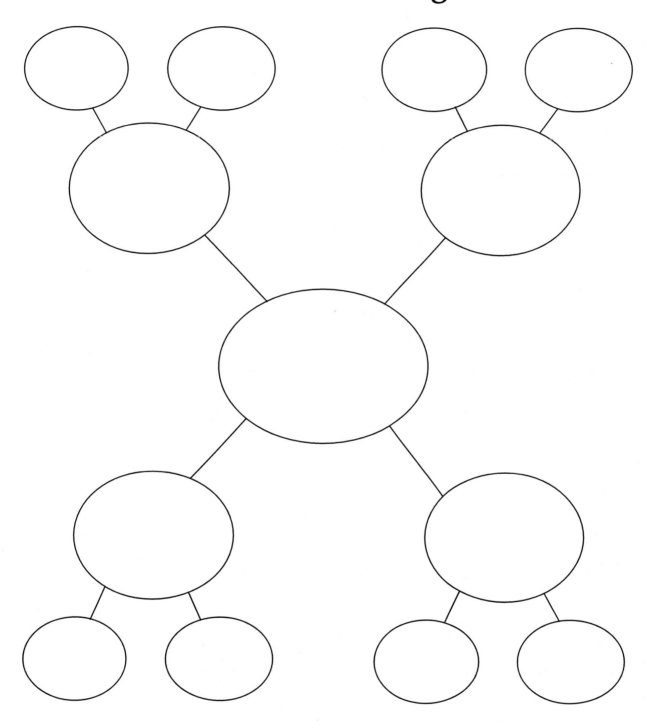

Content-Area Research Strategies

Overview of Reference Materials

Almanacs

Published yearly, almanacs provide current information on a wide range of topics, from census results to world records. Examples: *World Almanac and Book of Facts, The Time Almanac* (formerly the *Information Please Almanac).*

Atlases

Book of maps, either with or without text. Can be local (*Atlas of Alameda Co., California*) general (*Oxford Atlas of the World*), or on a specific subject (*Historical Maps of North America, Rand McNally Atlas of the Earth's Resources*).

Biographical Indexes

Brief articles about people who are important in particular fields. Some indexes are general, others focus on specific groups. Examples: *Who's Who, Encyclopedia of World Biography, The Penguin Biographical Dictionary of Women, Webster's Biographical Dictionary, The Dictionary of Literary Biography.*

Dictionaries

A dictionary gives definitions and spellings of words, arranged in alphabetical order. Some dictionaries provide definitions of words in one language. Examples: *Webster's Collegiate Dictionary, The American Heritage Dictionary, Le Petit Robert.* Some translate one language into another. Example: *HarperCollins French-English/English-French Dictionary.* Specialized dictionaries give definitions of technical terms in a specific field. Examples: *Dictionary of Computer Terms, Concise Oxford Dictionary of Politics.*

Specialized dictionaries can be found on dozens of subjects. Check with the reference librarian to find one for your topic.

Directories

Directories provide contact information for specific groups, people, or organizations. They often also provide brief summaries of a group or organization. Telephone directories for different areas can also be helpful resources. Examples: *Congressional Yellowbook, Literary Market Place.*

Encyclopedias (General)

Encyclopedias give an overview of a lot of topics. Because they include so many topics, they don't cover anything very deeply. Still, encyclopedia articles are a good way to get a general idea of a topic. Use the index (often in a separate volume) to find your topic. Examples: *New Encyclopaedia Britannica, Encyclopedia Americana.*

Encyclopedias (Specialized)

As the name suggests, these encyclopedias cover just one subject. Examples: *The Oxford Companion to English Literature, Encyclopedia of World Cultures, Encyclopedia of Science & Technology.*

Gazetteers

Gazetteers give the names of places and their locations, in alphabetical order. Locations are usually given in latitude and longitude. Examples: *Chambers World Gazetteer: An A-Z of Geographical Information; Omni Gazetteer of the United States of America.*

Government Publications

The U.S. government produces and distributes information on many subjects. These publications are a valuable source of information, particularly for reliable statistics. Topics include employment figures, census data, and so forth. Example: *The Statistical Abstracts of the United States.*

Guidebooks

Often designed for travelers, guidebooks offer information and directions. They are useful for finding more detailed information about an area than geography books or atlases offer. Examples: *National Geographic's Guide to the National Parks of the United States, Lake Baikal Guidebook.*

Handbooks/Manuals

These books gather and organize critical information in a given field. Some give data and equations needed for scientific experiment; some give criteria for making medical diagnoses, or prescribing medication. Examples: *Diagnostic and Statistical Manual of Mental Disorders, Fourth Edition; Physicians Desk Reference; A Manual for Writing Term Papers.*

Thesaurus

A book that tells you what words are similar in meaning. Use one of these to expand your list of search terms. Example: *Roget's Thesaurus.*

Materials Evaluation Checklist

1. Is the date of the source current enough for my topic? Yes ___ No ___

2. Is the material relevant to my topic? Yes ___ No ___

3. Is the author a credible source, with authority and expertise in the field? Yes ___ No ___

4. Is the publisher a reliable, unbiased source of material on this topic? Yes ___ No ___

5. Is evidence provided to support all statements? Yes ___ No ___

6. Is the coverage suitable for my topic? Yes ___ No ___

7. Does the information agree with what I already know about the subject? Yes ___ No ___

8. Does the information make sense? Yes ___ No ___

9. Is the language reasonable and objective? Yes ___ No ___

Content-Area Research Strategies

Bibliographic Information Checklist

The left-hand column below explains the details required for the most common types of resources. The right-hand column gives an example of each type.

Book

Author (authors, if more than one):	Hannah Holmes
<u>Title</u> (underlined)	<u>The Secret Life of Dust: From the Cosmos to the Kitchen Counter, the Big Consequences of Little Things</u>
Place of Publication:	New York
Publisher:	John Wiley & Sons, Inc.
Copyright date:	2001
Pages:	239

Encyclopedia

Author (if given):	Peter Goodman
"Title of article" (in quotation marks):	"The Art of Negotiation"
<u>Name of encyclopedia</u> (underlined):	<u>Encyclopedia Hibernica</u>
Edition (year):	2002
Volume number:	1
Pages:	82–83

Magazine, Newspaper, or Journal Article

Author of article:	Laura Dabundo
"Title of article" (in quotation marks)	"'The Voice of the Mute': Wordsworth and the Ideology of Romantic Silences."
<u>Name of magazine</u> (underlined)	<u>Christianity and Literature</u>
Volume number:	43:1
Date:	1995
Pages:	21–35

Bibliographic Information Checklist *(continued)*

Video or Film

<u>Title</u> (underlined):   <u>Do</u>
<u>the Right Thing</u>

Director:
Spike Lee

Distributor:
Forty Acres and a Mule Filmworks

Year released:
1989

Television Program

"Episode title" (in quotation marks):
"Provenance"

<u>Show title</u> (underlined):   <u>The</u>
<u>X-Files</u>

Producer:
Fox. WXIA, Atlanta

Air date: 3
March 2002

Internet

Author's name (if available):
William J. Duiker

"Title of document":
"Ho Chi Minh"

Source organization (if available):
Encarta Online Encyclopedia. Microsoft

Corporation.

<URL> (between angle brackets):
<http://encarta.msn.com>

Date accessed: 26
Sept. 2001

Standard Outline Format

I. _____

   A. _____

      1. _____

      2. _____

   B. _____

      1. _____

      2. _____

II. _____

   A. _____

      1. _____

      2. _____

   B. _____

      1. _____

      2. _____

III. _____

   A. _____

      1. _____

      2. _____

   B. _____

      1. _____

      2. _____

IV. _____

   A. _____

      1. _____

      2. _____

   B. _____

      1. _____

      2. _____

Content-Area Research Strategies

Revising Checklist

Use this checklist to make sure your essay is complete.

Big-Picture Issues

___ Does the whole paper make sense?

___ Does it express my main idea?

___ Is the writing pattern appropriate for the topic?

___ Do I have an introduction? supporting paragraphs? a conclusion?

___ Does each paragraph serve a purpose in the essay as a whole?

___ Are the paragraphs in a logical order?

___ Do the paragraphs flow smoothly?

___ Have I used transition words to link paragraphs?

___ Is the paper interesting?

Fine-Print Issues

___ Does my introduction present the main idea of the essay?

___ Do I have a well-developed paragraph for each topic?

___ Does each paragraph contain one idea, and only one?

___ Do I use facts and details to support my statements?

___ Do I use transition words to link my paragraphs?

___ Do I present ideas and information in a logical sequence?

___ Do I present ideas and information clearly?

___ Does my conclusion wrap up the points I made in the essay?

___ Does my essay follow my outline?

___ Have I included all the topics I had identified?

Editing and Proofreading Checklist

___ Have I checked my spelling?

___ Are all my sentences clear and complete?

___ Do I have any run-on sentences?

___ Do I have any sentence fragments?

___ Do nouns and verbs agree in number?

___ Have I used punctuation correctly?

___ Are all quotations handled appropriately (in quotation marks or set as block quotations)?

___ Do I have a complete citation for every quotation?

___ Is my choice of words clear and effective?

___ Are my verb tenses consistent?

___ Have I eliminated unnecessary words?

___ Have I checked for long words where short ones could be used?

Overview of Works Cited Page

Tips

- Head the page "Works Cited."
- List all sources you used to prepare your paper.
- Arrange the sources in alphabetical order by author's last name.
- List authors last name first so they are easy to find.
- Underline the names of whole works.
- Put the names of partial works "in quotation marks."
- Start each entry at the left margin. Don't put the author on one line, the title on the next, and so forth. Just keep going until you reach the end of the line. Then indent the second line and continue. This makes it easier to see where one entry ends and the next one starts.
- If no author name is given, start with the title of the book, article, and so forth.

Books

Book, One Author

Author (last name, first name). <u>Title of the book</u>. City: Publisher, date of publication.

Simpson, Bart. <u>How to Succeed in School</u>. Springfield: Krusty Publishing, 2002.

Book, Two Authors

First author (last name, first name), and Second author (first name, last name). <u>Title of the book</u>. City: Publisher, date of publication.

Burns, Charles, and Maggie Simpson. <u>A Partnership Made in Heaven</u>. Capitol City: Burns Worldwide, 2000.

Book, No Author Named

<u>Title</u>. City: Publisher, date of publication.

<u>The Simpsons Dictionary</u>. Shelbyville: Amadopolis Aristole Press, 2003.

Encyclopedia

Author of Article (if given). "Article Title." <u>Encyclopedia Title</u>, Edition Date.

Flanders, Ned. "Good Neighbors." <u>Encyclopedia D'oh</u>. 2003 ed.

Articles

Magazine

Author (last name first). "Article Title." <u>Name of Magazine</u>. Date: Page(s).

Van Houten, Milhouse. "My Buddy Bart." <u>Clog Dancing Times</u>. 6 Jun 2001: 17.

Newspaper

Author (last name first). "Article Title." <u>Name of newspaper</u>. (date): edition if available, section, page number(s).

Skinner, Seymour. "Hair Care for Today's Man." <u>Springfield Times</u>. 8 Dec 2000: 1.

Television and Movies

Television program

"Title of Episode or Segment." Credit (Performer or author). <u>Title of Program</u>. Name of Network. Call letters (if any), City of Local Station (if any). Broadcast Date.

"Lost Our Lisa." Mat Groening. <u>The Simpsons</u>. FOX. 17 May 1998.

Movie

<u>Title</u>. Director. Distributor, Year.

<u>Who Shot Mr. Burns?</u> Dir. Waylon Smithers. Sector 7G Films, 1999.

Content-Area Research Strategies

Overview of Works Cited Page *(continued)*

On-line Resources

Web site

Creator's name (if given), last name first. <u>Web Page Title</u>. Date of latest update. Institution or organization. Date of access. <URL network address>.

Wiggum, Ralph. <u>Eat Paste</u>. 8 Nov. 2002. Springfield Elementary School. 6 Jan. 2003. <http://www.eatpaste.edu/recipes.html>.

Article in On-line Reference

"Article Title." <u>Web Page Title</u>. Date of latest update. Institution or organization. Date of access. <URL network address>.

"The Simpsons as Social Commentary." <u>D'oh Online</u>. Mar. 2002. Encyclopedia D'oh. 29 Mar. 2002 <http://www.doh.com/satire.html>.

Article in an On-line Magazine

Author's name (if given). "Title of Article." <u>Name of Magazine</u> Date of Publication. Date of Access <URL network address>.

Borton, Wendell. "Travel Sickness as a Metaphor for Life." <u>Bus Times</u> 1 May 1999. 2 May 1999 <http://www.bigyellowbus.com/fieldtrip.html>.

PART VI
Teacher's Guide

Part I: The Research Topic

Students' answers to most of the assignments in this section will vary. Sample answers are given as general guidance. You may also want to use the sample answers as prompts for students who find the activities challenging.

Lesson 1: Getting Organized

Application

You may want students to use an actual research assignment for this activity. If so, make sure students know the due date for the assignment, and have them put that date in the timetable grid.

Student answers will vary, but the grids should resemble this one.

Assignment date: 10/3/04
Due date: 10/31/04

Step-by-step research and writing	% of time	date you will finish
Step 1: Planning the process	5%	10/5/04
Step 2: Choosing a topic	10%	10/8/04
Step 3: Finding the focus for your topic	20%	10/14/04
Step 4: Gathering information	25%	10/21/04
Step 5: Preparing to write	10%	10/22/04
Step 6: Writing and revising	30%	10/31/04

Lesson 2: Choosing a Topic

Application

Student answers will vary; a sample response is shown below.

- The article says the reeds made "wedge-shaped" marks; that's hard to visualize. I wonder what they looked like? And if all the marks were wedges, how could they tell which mark stood for what?
- The article explained the meaning of "cuneiform," but "hieroglyphic" is a pretty strange word, too. I wonder why Egyptian writing is called "hieroglyphic."
- I've seen hieroglyphics; some of them looked like drawings, not writing.
- I wonder what the writing on the Rosetta Stone said.

Possible Research Topics: "Cuneiform Writing," "Egyptian Hieroglyphics," "Deciphering the Rosetta Stone."

Lesson 3: Finding a Focus

The research question can also be used to evaluate the focus of the topic. If the question uses the word "and" more than once—e.g., "Who were the gods of ancient Egypt, and what did people believe about the Afterlife, and how did they prepare for the Afterlife?"—then the topic is not focused enough. This topic could form the basis for three research papers, not just one.

You may wish to allow students to choose their own topic from the list, or you may wish to assign the topic that is most applicable to your subject area. Students may need to read some background information first, either in their textbooks or in an encyclopedia, in order to narrow the topic.

Topic: The Rain Forest
Who is responsible for rain forest loss?
What kind of rain forest, tropical or temperate?
When did deforestation become a problem?
Where are rain forests found?
Why are the rain forests getting smaller?

How does loss of rain forests affect the rest of the world?

Focused topic: "How has deforestation in Brazil since 1980 affected the rest of the world?"

Topic: Ancient Rome
Will I look at Romans in general, or one famous Roman, such as Julius Caesar or Nero?
What are some of the Roman Empire's most famous achievements?
Will I look at the entire period of Roman history, or focus on one period—e.g., the Roman Republic, the Imperial Age?
Will I look at the entire Roman Empire, or just one part?
Why did the Romans build roads?
How did the Romans rule such a huge empire before the days of computers and fast transportation, like cars, planes, and trains?

Focused topic: "How did building a road system throughout the empire make Rome strong?"

Topic: The Printing Press
Who really invented movable type, Gutenberg or Pi Cheng, of China?
What aspect of printing will I look at—the physical process, or the results of having printed material available?
When—1040 in China, or 1450 in Europe?
Will I look at printing all over the world, or just in China, or just in Europe?
Why was printing so important?
How did printing affect European society?

Focused topic: "How did Gutenberg's introduction of movable type in 1450 affect European society?"

Topic: Number Systems
Who first used numbers?
What types of number systems are there, besides decimal?
When did the number system we use now take its current form?
Where did number systems originate?
Why do we call our numbers "indo-arabic"?
How did specific number systems work?

Focused topic: "How did the Romans add and subtract without a place value system?"

Part II: The Research Process

Lesson 4: Identify the Key Concepts

Student answers will vary. A sample answer is shown below.

Application

KEY CONCEPTS

Pros
self-assessment
check for understanding
preparation for next day's activities
study for tests
complete assignments not finished in class
reinforce concepts
gain experience with skill
parents expect it

Cons
busywork
takes too long
interferes with work, clubs, sports, social life, family life
overburdens kids

Lesson 5: Overview of Resources

This lesson gives a brief overview of print resources and the Internet as a research resource. You may wish to tell students that there are also other types of resources: letters, diaries, photographs, paintings, movies, videos, audio recordings, and so forth. However, few of these resources are accessible, or appropriate, at this level.

For students who need a review of what different reference resources contain, a reproducible Overview of Reference Materials is included on page 104.

Application

You may wish to allow students to choose their own topic from the list, or you may wish to assign the topic that is most applicable to your subject area. If library time is scheduled, have students identify specific resources for the research plan, not just general types of resources.

Research Topic: The Cherokee Trail of Tears: 1838–1839

My Research Plan:

1. Background information: textbook, encyclopedia
2. Subject-specific information: books on the subject
3. Supporting information: historical atlases
4. Other: newspapers from the 1800s

Research Topic: Mass Media: Images of Women in Advertising

My Research Plan:

1. Background information: encyclopedia, almanacs
2. Subject-specific information: periodical articles
3. Supporting information: books, popular magazines
4. Other: Internet

Research Topic: Francis Crick and Jim Watson: Discovering the Double Helix of DNA

My Research Plan:

1. Background information: encyclopedia, textbook, biographical index
2. Subject-specific information: books on the subject
3. Supporting information: articles
4. Other: Internet

Research Topic: Famous Mathematicians of the Twentieth Century

My Research Plan:

1. Background information: math encyclopedia, biographical index
2. Subject-specific information: books, articles
3. Supporting information: Internet
4. Other: math dictionary

Lesson 6: Evaluating Resources

A reproducible version of the Materials Evaluation Checklist is provided on page 106.

Lesson 7: Evaluating Internet Sources

Application

Student responses will vary. A sample answer is given below.

✓ 1. http://www.oilspillcommission.gov

✓ 2. http://www.fakr.noaa.gov/oil/default.htm

? 3. http://www.friendsofthecoast.org

X 4. http://www.what~spill.name

Lesson 8: Reading for Research

You may wish to assign texts to students so that they can practice the skills taught in this lesson.

Student answers to the application sections will vary. Sample answers:

SCANNING

This article is about painting in Egypt, and why artists drew people the way they did.

SKIMMING

The main points are we know about ancient Egypt from Egyptian art; their drawings show people at a strange angle; they weren't trying to draw what they saw, but what they knew was there; rules developed to make sure tomb paintings were complete.

Lesson 9: Recording Bibliographic Information

At this point, students don't need to worry about which citation style to use in the bibliography, as all styles require the same basic information. A reproducible version of the Bibliographic Information Checklist is included on page 107.

Lesson 10: Preparing Bibliography Cards

Application

Author: Lisa Beyer	Source #1
Article title: "Roots of Rage"	Type: Article
Magazine: <u>Time</u>	
Pages: 40–42	
Date: 1 Oct. 2001	

Author: T. Midge	Source #2
Article title: "Powwows"	Type: Encyclopedia
Encyclopedia: <u>Encyclopedia of North American Indians</u>	
Year: 1997	

Lesson 11: Taking Notes

Application

Answers will vary. Possible answers:

Main idea, paragraph 1: Only free adult men with Athenian parents (451 B.C.E.—15% of population) could be citizens and vote; women, slaves, and foreigners could not. Relevant to topic? Yes

Main idea, paragraph 2: Even being a citizen didn't mean security. If enough people (6,000) voted to make him go, a citizen could be forced to leave Athens for 10 years. Relevant to topic? Yes

Lesson 12: Preparing Content Cards

Application

Answers will vary. Sample answers:

Abuses	Source #2
	page 17
Some indentured servants were treated badly; they were overworked, underfed, even branded by their owners.	

Advantages	Source #2
	page 17
Under a kind master, an indentured servant could be treated well and could become independent when the service ended.	

Lesson 13: Plagiarism and Quoting

Some students may be interested in the origin of the word *plagiarism*. It comes from the Latin word *plagiare*, "to kidnap." Plagiarism is like kidnapping someone else's work.

Application

Answers will vary. Sample answer:

Nixon's Hypocrisy	Source #6
	page 111
"However, new information then came to me which persuaded me that there was a real possibility that some of these charges were true, and suggesting further that there had been an effort to conceal the facts both from the public, from you, and from me." —Richard M. Nixon	

Lesson 14: Organizing Your Notes

Application

Answers will vary. Here is a possible sequence:

11. father thought writing wouldn't pay, wanted more practical career for Langston
2. born February 1, 1902, Joplin, Missouri
5. at 13 moved to Lincoln, Illinois, to live with his mother, her husband
14. soon dropped out of Columbia engineering program, continued to write
1. full name: James Langston Hughes
4. raised by his grandmother until he was 13
8. attended Central High School in Cleveland, Ohio
10. after high school spent a year in Mexico with father

7. began writing poetry in eighth grade, was named class poet

12. father paid tuition at Columbia University to study engineering

3. parents divorced when he was small, father moved to Mexico

9. 1920: finished high school

6. family eventually settled in Cleveland, Ohio

13. spent a year at Columbia University

Part III: Writing the Paper

Lesson 15: Choosing a Writing Pattern

Application

Answers will vary. One possible choice would be a chronological-order essay.

Lesson 16: Developing the Outline

A reproducible version of the Standard Outline Format is provided on page 109.

Application

Sample answer:

I. Childhood
   A. born February 1, 1902, Joplin, Missouri
   B. parents divorced when he was small, father moved to Mexico
      1. raised by his grandmother until he was 13
      2. at 13 moved to Lincoln, Illinois to live with mother, her husband
      3. family eventually settled in Cleveland, Ohio

II. Education
   A. attended Central High School in Cleveland, Ohio
   B. 1920: finished high school
   C. father thought writing wouldn't pay, wanted more practical career for Langston
      1. father paid tuition at Columbia University to study engineering

2. Langston spent a year at Columbia University

3. dropped out of Columbia engineering program, continued to write

Lesson 17: Writing the First Draft

You may want to emphasize the importance of content rather than mechanics in the first draft stage. There may be many drafts for any project.

Lesson 18: Handling Quoted Material

This section describes using the Modern Language Association (MLA) parenthetic citation style. This style is much easier to use than footnotes or endnotes. If you want your students to use a different style for citations, you may wish to customize this text to suit your needs.

Application

Answers will vary. Possible answer:

Because of the Watergate scandal, President Nixon was forced to resign. It started with a burglary in Washington, D.C. The trial of the burglars "led to disclosures that seemed to link the burglary and other events to the White House" (Baker 110).

Lesson 19: Revising and Editing the Draft

Reproducible versions of the Revising Checklist and the Editing and Proofreading Checklist are provided on pages 110 and 111.

Lesson 20: Preparing the Bibliography

As noted earlier, the bibliographic style described here is MLA style. If you want your students to use another style, customize the text to match that style. A reproducible version of the Overview of Works Cited Page is provided on page 112.

You will notice that the text refers only to underlining bibliographic elements, not using italics. Although many word processors make italicizing easy, letters in computer-generated italics can sometimes be difficult to read. MLA recommends underlining for clarity, but italics are also acceptable. Direct your students to use the approach you prefer.

Application

DeMente, Boye. <u>The Whole Japan Book.</u> Phoenix, AZ: Phoenix Book Publishers, 1983.

<u>Japan Crafts</u>. Sept. 12 2002. Japan Atlas. 3 Nov. 2002. <http://www.jinjapan.org/atlas/crafts/craft_fr.html>.

Zurlo, Tony. <u>Japan: Superpower of the Pacific.</u> Parsippany, NJ: Dillon Press, 1991.

Part IV: Excerpts

This section includes four sets of excerpts, one set each for Science, Math, Social Studies, and English. Each set consists of four excerpts on the same topic, or on closely related topics. Each excerpt in the set includes slightly different information. In several sets, each excerpt is from a different type of research resource: books, articles, encyclopedias, dictionaries, the Internet, and so on. Some of the excerpts have been created expressly for this book, complete with bibliographical information. This bibliographic information was intentionally left in an incorrect format so that students can format it correctly. Be aware that not all the references given here are valid; they are for practice use only.

You may wish to have students use the set of excerpts that is most related to your subject area as they go through the lessons in this book. Alternatively, you may wish to use the excerpts after students have completed the lessons, to practice the skills they have learned with a controlled set of materials.

Excerpt Set A: Glaciers

Excerpt Set B: Famous Mathematicians

Excerpt Set C: Ancient Civilizations

Excerpt Set D: S. E. Hinton

Part V: Graphic Organizers

This section contains reproducible copies of the graphic organizers and checklists used in the lessons. You can make copies of these organizers and checklists for students to use as they prepare an actual research paper.